INTO THE I
JU

An invitation to stand in the counsel of the Judge of All the Earth

By Jess Gjerstad

ACKNOWLEDGEMENTS

There are many people I want to acknowledge who greatly helped me in writing this book: First, I am grateful for my parents, Kerry and Carolyn who raised me and supported me in my ministry.

I also want to thank spiritual "moms" and "dads" who sowed into my life with prayer and understanding such as Mary Lou Schutz, Pam Hasaladen, Paul Anderson, along with Todd and Mary Bullock who strengthened me on my journey in prayer.

I am also grateful for people such as Hal Linhardt, Laurie Ditto, Dave and Ivy Anderson along with so many others that I currently serve with at the International House of Prayer in Kansas City.

I am also grateful to Heather Griffith, Michelle Smith, and others who helped me edit and proof read this book.

TABLE OF CONTENTS

INTRODUCTION

Eternal judgment is a foundational doctrine found in scripture, but it is one of the least touched subjects in this generation. Some proclaim that God's final judgment was only at the cross-and therefore, God does not judge any more. Meanwhile, others proclaim the coming of God's judgment because of their anger over the moral filth in society. Many in the Church are confused. As the result, our nation is at a crisis over the righteousness, justice, and the nature of God's judgment.

For example, September 11 was a crisis moment in the Church and in America as planes slammed into New York and Washington with cameras rolling. The following Sunday, the churches in America were completely packed out as people sought out answers from God's Word along with comfort and understanding.

On the national stage, some preachers rose up and proclaimed the disaster as a judgment of God and the need for personal and national repentance. Meanwhile, others proclaimed the compassion, consolation, and comfort of God to a traumatized nation in the midst of tragedy. Still many others in the wake of 9-11 proclaimed it as an act of evil and encouraged us to stand up to defend freedom. All of these perspectives were biblically correct, but also incomplete.

The resulting collective message from the evangelical church in America was very confusing. As the result, many concluded that the Church was very confused, and mostly irrelevant. Church attendance plummeted in the following weeks and years. Inevitably, more lives were lost eternally because of this lack of clarity.

In wrestling with the issue of God's judgments, I am not here to necessarily say one event (like 9-11 that killed roughly 3,000 people and caused tremendous sorrow and pain) was clearly "God's judgment"- while ignoring many smaller events.

For example, 30,000+ people are killed on our roadways in accidents every year in the United States. Can we trace these small tragedies to God's judgment? God's justice and wisdom in specific incidents is difficult to discern. Only eternity will reveal the wisdom of God in permitting difficult and painful events.

I am also not here to single out one type of sinner or group of sinners as worse than another type of sinner. Jesus specifically warned against this behavior in Luke 13:1-5. For example, New Orleans (that got devastated by Hurricane Katrina in 2005) is not necessarily more ungodly than Seattle or Detroit. Indeed, we were all sinners from birth. We are also in danger of reaping the horrific consequences of sin if we do not repent individually and corporately as community, Church, and nation.

Not all judgment is negative. Indeed, much of the Church is praying for the justice of God to break in on a regular basis in the form of miraculous healing (judgment against sickness), deliverance against demonic oppression (judgment against demons), and salvation of loved ones. Then there is the judgment seat of Christ with the opportunity for eternal rewards that touch our deepest desires.

I am convinced that the Church must know the heart of the Judge to be able to instruct many in the midst of crisis that is coming. Daniel prophesied that those who are wise in that day would be able to instruct many. This book is an attempt to make a template to bring clarity to understand the different layers of God's emotions related to the administration of justice in time and eternity. The story line around "Caring Christian" at the beginning of each chapter give a realistic example of how the hidden judgment activity of God affects the everyday life of believers like you and me while life goes on, "business as usual".

Wrestling with God over the issue of justice often involves a lot of heartache and pain. Why does God allow "bad things" to happen to good people? When will God avenge the wrong that I suffered? The pains of the injustice we have suffered distort our perception of God's justice.

We must seek to understand the heart of Jesus as judge. What would have happened if before 9-11, the Church had already wrestled to understand the heart of

God as judge? What if the Church had proclaimed a united message of the heart of Jesus in the midst of sorrow, and tragedy? When the next personal, national, or global crisis happens, will we have a biblical template to help people process the frightening, tragic, and painful events? It is my prayer that there will be many who are wise to preserve life by their words in the midst of coming crisis.

Chapter 1:

Is God a Judge?

There are two kinds of people: those who say to God, 'Thy will be done' and those to whom God says, 'All right, then, have it your own way.' -C.S. Lewis

Caring Christian bounded through Wise Willy's front door, face aglow. "I've got great news! This has to be one of the greatest days of my life!"

"What's the good news?" asked Wise Willy.

"Swindler Sam selected me to be a business partner with him in the new company he started, called Mischievous Marketing, a specialized training company to produce high-performance leaders and businesses using the latest expertise in human psychology, hidden wisdom, and market understanding."

"Are you sure this is a good idea?" asked Wise Willy. "God's Word is clear on the issues of deception and theft."

"Oh come on, Wise Willy" Caring Christian retorted. "I don't think that God minds. It looks like God is blessing me for my new-found commitment to Jesus."

"Be careful, Caring Christian," said Wise Willy with a hint of sorrow.

Caring Christian responded, "I know that God cares for all people. I also see that the Bible talks about judgment, but that appears to be done away with at the cross. How can God still be a judge? I don't see the judgments falling on the wicked today."

Caring Christian continued, "What really turned me off to Christianity beforehand was how the Church preached hellfire and judgment. It seemed like they were doing it to intimidate and manipulate people into following a set of religious rules and rituals. Yuck! Meanwhile, I would see church folk do the exact same things they preached against and there was no judgment that hit them."

"Just because you don't see the judgment doesn't mean that God is not a judge" said Wise Willie. "While God is slow to anger and delights in showing mercy, you need to remember that God is also righteous and just."

Does God judge? Moral relativity vs. moral absolutes

Sadly, Caring Christian's understanding of God's justice reflects the views of millions of Christians in the Church today. Many view the judgments of God as a thing of the past and outdated. They ignore scriptures such as Malachi 3:6, Hebrews 13:5, and other passages that talk

10

about how God's character and nature do not change. The same God of the Old Testament who judges and brings redemption is the same God of the New Testament who judges and brings redemption.

The writer of Hebrews affirmed that understanding eternal judgment is a foundational doctrine (Hebrews 6:1). The writer affirms that we will all one day face the judgment (9:27). The great creeds of the Church affirm Jesus is the Judge. The Apostle's Creed (repeated in many congregations every Sunday) states:

He (Jesus) will come again to judge the living and the dead.

Yet in our postmodern society, the doctrine of God's righteous judgment is under attack from groups within and outside the Church. We can easily point to the troubles outside the Church pretty easy with moral relativism. However, the underlying humanistic belief system has infiltrated the Church, among those who profess Jesus Christ as their Lord.

"Justice" has been defined many ways by many people. For example, Webster's dictionary lists about a dozen definitions for "justice" ranging from a legal term of rewards and punishments to a moral term of equity, righteousness, and fairness. Most of us are not familiar with the term "justice" until we experience "injustice".

For many of you, the first encounter with injustice was with a sibling who took something from you. For many others, the first encounter was when friends or playmates cheated at a game, or when the other kid took the ball that you were playing with. Others were introduced to injustice in a much more painful way such as discrimination based on skin color, or realizing that your parents had a favorite child-not named you. Some of you were introduced to injustice in much more traumatic and devastating ways.

In any case, we live in a world filled with injustice. Very often people with wealth, resources, or power misuse them to oppress the poor. Who can forget the injustice and controversy associated with Martin Luther King, Rodney King, or Trayvon Martin?

Even as individuals suffer from the effects of injustice, whole cultures and international relations have been marked and distorted due to corporate injustice. For example, Native Americans still hold deep bitterness towards the U.S. government due to Sand Creek, Wounded Knee, and other massacres. Meanwhile these events of the 19th century are told positively in "how the West was Won" in U.S. history. China, North and South Korea, and other nations still hold deep bitterness towards the Japanese for atrocities committed in World War II. In extreme cases, it is related to genocide. For example, the Armenians in Turkey were massacred in 1915 by the government, and the perpetrators seemingly got away with murder.

In the midst of the horror of extreme injustice, many have cried out, "*Where was God in the midst of the injustice?*" God could have easily stopped the massacre, the torment and the pain, yet he chose not to. Bitter anger towards the perpetrators was directed at God, who chose not to stop the pain. In some cases, the horror was so great and the bitter pain is so deep that it was easier to let the heart stay numb and cold. The alternative to feel emotion again is simply too painful.

Righteousness and justice: How are our views formed?

As little children, we tend to think in terms of morality only black and white until life appears to hit us with complex situations. A moral absolute is a belief that something is *always* right or wrong for people of all times, cultures, and seasons regardless of the situation. When we are little children, our parents or those in authority train us: Obey and you get rewarded. Disobedience brings painful punishment. Since no one likes pain, we learn as children that obedience means rewards and freedom from pain. We all grew up with punished disobedience and rewarded obedience.

Since scripture tells us that man is made in the image of God (Genesis 1:26), we presume that obedience to God brings a reward and that disobedience brings some painful negative consequence(s). When we were young, many of us learned the Ten Commandments-or at least heard of them. These are God's moral absolutes-obedience brings blessing, disobedience brings judgment. God trained a new nation in the wilderness to know what was right or wrong.

As teenagers and adults, we learn another dimension of how life works-that challenges child-hood beliefs our parents or authority figures taught us: Obedience to those in authority doesn't always bring a reward. Meanwhile we also learn that disobedience doesn't always bring an immediate punishment or consequences. Undoubtedly, we did something disobedient, "got away with it", and then later told the story to our friends.

These emotionally disillusioning experiences force us to rethink our morality, values, and sources of wisdom. As we develop more sophisticated ways of thinking, more questions arise: Why are people put into places of authority? Are they trustworthy? Why did God say, "You shall have no other gods" (Exodus 20:3)?

God addresses many of these questions in the narrative story lines of the Bible. God exalted David's Kingdom but brought down the kingdom of Saul. Song of Songs, Proverbs, and Ecclesiastes were written by the man who asked God for the gift of wisdom. (This request proved at that time that Solomon was already very wise but didn't know it.) The narratives invite us to understand God's ways and trust his leadership in the midst confusing situations.

However, there are times in life when right and wrong seem completely upside down: Biblical character qualities such as righteousness, humility, and obedience bring greater pressure and pain that is apparently unending. Meanwhile, vices such as self-centeredness, arrogance, and deceptive intimidation or manipulation bring greater ease and comfort to those around us. When obedience to God brings pain while sin brings temporary pleasure, questions of God's justice rise up at the emotional level: Is God truly just?

Confronting the ditch of lawlessness

In response to extremely painful and confusing situations, many in our society have gone from proclaiming moral absolutes to embracing moral relativism. Underlying moral relativism is self-centeredness: Life is about "me", what "I" want, and what "my" desires are.

Most moral relativists take a stand-*"There are no moral absolutes"*. The only problem with this statement is that they just made the absolute claim that there are no absolute claims. More sophisticated moral relativists take a stand that there *may* (however unlikely) be some type of moral absolute standards out there, but it is impossible to absolutely prove them. Thus we are back to relativism-it's all about whatever is best for "me", "myself", and "I".

A close cousin to moral relativism is universalism. Universalism is the belief that eventually, all will end up reconciled to God and in heaven (including satan, who will not change). In universalism, all belief systems lead to heaven. Many preachers imply this error at funerals in an attempt to comfort a grieving family.

The net effect of this doctrine is to make the issues of justice and righteousness relative to the times and seasons we live in. This type of mindset "frees" people to do whatever is right- at least in their own eyes. Sadly, this ancient heresy is becoming practically popular in many branches of Christianity who profess Jesus.

Underlying this false doctrine is the false "Santa Claus" view of God. Growing up in a good Lutheran home, right before Christmas, my sister and I would get our time in sitting on Santa's lap and telling him what we wanted for Christmas. We would then wake up on Christmas Day and find that "Santa" had brought Christmas presents that we had asked for. All would be happy and well.

In approaching God in prayer, we often wrongly think that God is only like Santa Claus. We simply ask for whatever we wanted (in prayer) and then God is obliged (like a heavenly "Santa Claus") to give us what we wanted.

God is incredibly kind, wise, and good. However, he is not like Santa Claus who gives us everything we want. Sadly, when God doesn't give us whatever we wanted, out

14

of our bitter disappointment and hope deferred, we then trend towards practical atheism.

Another close cousin to moral relativism and universalism is the new "avant-garde" teaching on grace. Basically proponents of this new grace teaching believe that all judgment was taken care of at the cross of Jesus for believers and unbelievers. It is now simply a matter of understanding our identity in Christ and taking in this grace for us. Quoting select biblical texts, these modern grace teachers turn the grace of God into a license to be self-centered without eternal consequences. The understanding of eternal judgment is thrown into the ditch as rather "irrelevant" if we understand "grace".

Many, who hear this distorted grace message, find this teaching initially seems very refreshing. Many have grown up with a performance mentality thinking that we need to perform to be accepted by God. A grace message based upon identity is very liberating from legalism.

What makes the new "hyper-grace" teaching so dangerous is that it then pulls us into the opposite ditch called lawlessness. While our actions can never save us, we differentiate identities by attributes. If it sounds like a pig, loves mud like a pig, and in every other way looks like a pig, do we call it a pig?

In the same way, those who belong to Jesus look, sound, and act different than what other people who are self-centered do. They act differently and look different than those who do not know Jesus- especially in times of great crisis. The biblical grace message is filled with power from God to make us represent Jesus with increasing fullness. Grace is based on our identity in Jesus and our great worth to God.

The biblical identity in Christ message sets us free from the ditch of "performance mentality" related to legalism (which is good). God graciously offers us a new identity in Jesus Christ. Our value to God is not based upon our performance, but upon what Jesus did on the cross. The biblical identity message also emphasizes that God is progressively transforming us to look and live more like Jesus.

The net effect of distorted teaching on grace is lawlessness- I can do whatever I want when I want, and the "grace of God" will cover my sin. All of the judgment was taken care of at the cross- and I can do whatever I want. The full destructive fruit of this teaching is not yet fully evident. Yet history and a careful analysis of scripture indicate that this leads to destruction. This false grace message is related to Greek mindset that whatever is spiritual is separated from whatever I do in the physical and material realm.

Sadly, many are going to be shocked in a horrible way when they stand before Jesus on that last Judgment Day. Expecting affirmation, they hear something else. Scripture warns:

As the body without the spirit is dead, so faith without works is dead. (James 2:26)

Jesus plainly warned:

"Not everyone who says to me, 'Lord, Lord' will enter the kingdom of heaven, but only he who does the will of my Father who is in heaven. Many will say to me on that day, 'Lord, Lord, did we not prophesy in your name and in your name drive out demons and perform many miracles? Then I will tell them plainly, 'I never knew you. Away from me, you evildoers!'" (Matthew 7:21-23)

In that day, they will understand that Jesus is the Righteous Judge-and it will be too late to change the final assessment. God's judgment is absolute and final with no appeals.

Judge not?

Many postmodernists embrace universalism and relativism because of the "lessons learned" over history and their own personal experiences. No one likes to feel "judged" when they are dishonored or humiliated even in a peer relationship context. Therefore, they take the words of Jesus out of context and say "judge not".

World history is littered with examples of gross corporate injustice, with a large amount of it based on religious or political systems. For example, the Catholic Church condemned Galileo for scientifically challenging their dogmatic theological interpretations of the Bible- such as the belief that the sun orbited the earth. The resulting confrontation led to an adversarial relationship between inquiry in seeking out truth systematically (scientific method) and theology. Only recently did the Catholic Church issue a statement clearing Galileo of heresy[1].

Even in American history, we find much prejudice and discrimination based upon culture and skin color resulting in much pain. For example, much was written about in our culture on "how the West was won" related to settlers against the "savage" and "pagan" natives. Another example is the enslavement of Africans by British, American, and other European powers. Still another example is the discrimination against Japanese Citizens in World War II out of fear that they would conspire with Japan and commit treason against the United States. A much more recent example is the hatred some Muslim communities experienced in the wake of the September 11th attacks.

In many cases, the prejudice and discrimination has been based upon religious and theological grounds: For example, the conquest of the West was theologically compared to Joshua conquering the land of Canaan[2]. Colonization and enslavement of people in Africa, and Asia was justified by European powers in the name of spreading "the gospel" to heathen cultures.

At the forefront of the abuse, was the misuse of the doctrine of hellfire and eternal judgment. This doctrine was used to intimidate people into conforming culturally and

---

[1] The Catholic Church exonerated Galileo in 1992. http://en.wikipedia.org/wiki/Galileo_affair
[2] Scott, Donald M. "The Religious Origins of Manifest Destiny." Divining America, TeacherServe©. National Humanities Center. 8/18/14 http://nationalhumanitiescenter.org/tserve/nineteen/nkeyinfo/mandestiny.htm>

religiously. To illiterate cultures becoming enslaved, this was extremely intimidating. Often the dominant culture would prevent the subservient culture from literacy and discovering what the Bible really says[3].

In nations such as Haiti, the native people group reacted to this enslavement by making a covenant with satan. To them, the God of the French Colonialists was oppressive and enslaving. Should we serve an oppressive, legalistic "God" the French Colonists preach or should we serve this other god that offers freedom to do whatever I want (even if it is harmful)? They had a voodoo ceremony in 1791 which launched a violent revolution in Haiti[4].

Using these historical examples of theological abuse and error, the emerging globalistic culture has now over-reacted into universalism and moral relativism in the hearts of many-particularly in the West. Any talk of the judgments of God is often viewed as narrow-minded and bigoted because of the terrible history of misusing this doctrine. Where is the God of justice?

Confronting legalism: Is God really like us?

A corporate consciousness of the fear of the LORD and the wrath of God is foundational to American society. Perhaps one of the most influential sermons ever preached in America was "Sinners in the hands of an Angry God" by Jonathan Edwards back in the Puritan days of 1741. This particular message and others like it ignited the 1st Great Awakening in the United States. The waves of revival and awakening that swept America and the United Kingdom set up many of our historic moral foundations. The fear of God was a key building block of society. However the scriptural understanding of the judgments of God became distorted over time.

Underlying our questions related to the justice of God was our own broken, sinful nature. Before sin distorted things, God gave humanity an awesome privilege and responsibility before all of creation:

---

[3] http://www.virtualjamestown.org/laws1.html
[4] http://en.wikipedia.org/wiki/Bois_Ca%C3%AFman

18

So God created man in his own image, in the image of God he created him; male and female he created them. (Genesis 1:27)

We were commissioned to "re-present" God to each other and all of creation. We were created to reveal the kindness, mercy, and righteousness of God to all of creation.

Much of our understanding about God comes from each other on both a conscious and a subconscious level. The Bible makes use of anthromorphism (describing God in human-like characteristics such as "The arm of the LORD" and the "eyes of the LORD") numerous times. We are wired subconsciously by our creator to believe that God is somewhat like us as human beings because we were created in his image.

We don't understand the awesome consequences of bearing God's image. Our role of image-bearers means that if we end up miss-judging a situation and then act, we send a non-verbal message that God does not have all the information and thus acts based on whatever his mood may be. How many of us have ever acted based on an evaluation and judgment, only to realize that it was completely wrong because we did not have all the information?

First, we often unintentionally misrepresent God towards other people simply based on how we are feeling that day. For example, woe to us or others if we are having a bad day. Since our moods change from day to day, we could erroneously conclude that God has "good days" and "bad days". Our natural, human conclusion related to God is to hope we catch God on a "good day". Woe to us if we should actually catch God on a "bad day" emotionally!

Secondly, we misrepresent God as simply someone who is most concerned about our ability to perform for him. To keep order, we have specific standards that people need to live up to. Imagine going to a doctor who is unqualified. Our nation adopted a free-market capitalistic system along with a representative democracy form of government. These societal foundations produce intensely performance-driven values within our society. The result is an evaluation-based society.

Due to our societal upbringing, we thus tend to judge each other by what they can offer us (based on their skill level and excellence). How many of us carry painful memories of getting rejected from something we wanted because we simply did not "make the grade" or "make the cut"?

Due to our responsibility to represent God to each other (Genesis 1:26-28), and many experiences of rejection, we unintentionally represent God as a judge who is constantly evaluating us-for the purpose of rejecting us. When we add the numerous passages about how God hates sin- we end up with a belief system that unless we perform to meet stringent legalistic standards (which are impossible to meet), we will get judged. The understanding of Jesus as a legalistic judge (waiting for a reason to stomp us out) from our upbringing is rather unnerving.

Thirdly, distortions of the anger and the wrath of God are also ingrained within our culture due to the misuse of authority and the apparent "inaction" of God. Why did God not bring openly visible judgment upon those in authority that were exposed for their hypocrisy (that ended up hurting a large number of people)? Undoubtedly, the misuse of institutional authority and systematic injustice played a role in this.

For example, a number of high-profile moral failures in the 1950s related to healing evangelists in the Church clearly exposed the institutional hypocrisy in even the most sacred of organizations. Dr. Martin Luther King with his nonviolent, Christ-centered preaching on systematic injustice helped give our nation a rude awakening. Like a child upset at waking up to the first day of school, the United States began to awake to the systematic injustice of the white "church culture" against African Americans, particularly in the southern states.

Beginning with the culture of rebellion and mistrust of institutional authority in the 1960s, the judgments and wrath of God became the focus of many jokes. Given the apparent lack of God's openly manifest judgment- people became emboldened in their rebellion. The entertainment industry makes fun of this tendency to make God in our own image in regards to the judgments of God. More than one Hollywood film has satirized the idea of God intervening in judgment. This all helps to promote universalism and moral relativism in the culture.

The Protesters at Onething 2012 and the irony of it all:

Every year, thousands of youth and young adults come to Kansas City to worship, pray, and seek the LORD at IHOP-KC's annual *Onething* conference. Tens of thousands of others tune in on-line. Of course with a conference this large focused on the supremacy of Jesus comes other groups determined to get their message across.

Peering out the window at *Onething Conference* in 2012, I could see the protesters holding signs on the street corner: One sign declared judgment on homosexuals. Another sign said, "GOD WILL JUDGE FALSE TEACHERS". This particular group from Kansas was known for picketing the funerals of soldiers who died defending our nation's freedom. This particular group believes God justly hates people caught in sin and that our nation deserves judgment for it. Yet they claimed to be born-again Christians. What about God's mercy?

Staring at them as they vented their anger and rage, I could not help but notice the irony. Earlier that same week, the homosexual community had been on the same street corner protesting the same conference accusing us of being bigoted and judgmental because we agreed with the Bible and did not bless their lifestyle. We had sent out some of our evangelistic friends to tell them about Jesus. Now, some of our leaders went out and talked to the newest group protesting our proclamation of Jesus.

In both cases, they were protesting related to the judgments of God. One group was angry because we were declaring the Jesus as a judge and warning of God's judgment upon those who refuse to repent and change their lifestyle. The other group was angry because we were preaching a message of redemption to even the vilest, and most broken through the justice of Jesus Christ.

God's word talks about the path of life (Proverbs 15:24; Psalm 16:11). On both sides of the highway of holiness are deep ditches. Could it be that both groups were viewing us (and the other group) from the ditches on the opposite sides of the path of life? In any case, the two protesting groups exposed a great vacuum in the conscience of our nation and the nations of the world: *We don't understand the heart of Jesus the judge.*

Can we understand the Judgments of the LORD?

The apparent actions (or mostly inaction) of God in judgment have left many perplexed: *Can we understand the judgments of God? What is the root of injustice anyway?* We presume that the root of injustice is relative to our interactions with people, while the Bible gives a totally different picture.

Throughout history, theologians, pastors, and lay people have said we can't understand the judgments of God. They used passages like this:

Oh the depth of the riches of the wisdom and knowledge of God! How unsearchable his judgments, and his paths beyond tracing out! Who has known the mind of the Lord? Or who has been his counselor? Who has ever given to God, that God should repay him? For from him and through him and to him are all things. To him be the glory forever! Amen. (Romans 11:33-36)

God's voice thunders in marvelous ways; he does great things beyond our understanding. (Job 37:5)

As the heavens are high and the earth is deep, so the hearts of kings are unsearchable. (Proverbs 25:3)

Do you not know? Have you not heard? The LORD is the everlasting God, the Creator of the ends of the earth. He will not grow tired or weary, and his understanding no one can fathom. (Isaiah 40:28)

Many may conclude, "If the heart of earthly kings are unsearchable, how much more the heart of the King of Kings?"

In many ways the specific judgment activity of God in a given situation is impossible to fully comprehend in this age. God interacts with seven billion human beings on a very personal level and corporate communal level in righteousness and justice. Exhaustively understanding God's justice becomes incredibly complex-beyond human understanding in this age.

In discussing the justice of God, we must also include the interactions of the angelic and demonic "races" with humanity and God our creator as well. Factoring in God's justice towards all of creation, the complexity becomes even more incredible (and beautiful) leaving us standing in awe of God like the apostle Paul.

Having said that exhaustively understanding the motivations behind God's judgments on all specific situations is impossible, is it possible to gain understanding of God's heart and wisdom behind his judgments? Scripture appears to give an invitation:

It is the glory of God to conceal a matter; to search out a matter is the glory of kings. (Proverbs 25:2)

"Call to me and I will answer you and tell you great and unsearchable things you do not know." (Jeremiah 33:3)

After this I looked, and there before me was a door standing open in heaven. And the voice I had first heard speaking to me like a trumpet said, "Come up here and I will show you what must take place after this." (Revelation 4:1)

Even Moses prophesied that God would make known some of his "secret things" so that the people could then follow God's instructions (Deuteronomy 29:29). Through the cross of Jesus and by the power of the Holy Spirit, we are invited into understanding the deepest mysteries of the universe found in the heart of our God. These mysteries are hidden in his word in plain view for all to see.

Getting to the heart of the matter:

The grace to understand God's justice and judgments will be a salvation issue for many. Scripture warns that at the end of the age there will be a great falling away, specifically related to bitterness and offense.

Make sure there is no man or woman, clan or tribe among you whose heart turns away from the LORD our God to go and worship the gods of those nations; make sure there is no root among you that produces such bitter poison (Deuteronomy 29:18)

The writer of Hebrews added insight into the danger of bitterness and offense:

See to it that no one misses the grace of God and that no bitter root grows up to cause trouble and defile many. See that no one is sexually immoral or is godless like Esau, who for a single meal sold his inheritance rights as the oldest son. Afterward, as you know, when he wanted to inherit this blessing, he was rejected. He could bring about no change of mind, though he sought the blessing with tears. (Hebrews 12:15-17)

Behind idolatry and lawlessness is the root of bitterness and offense towards God. In many cases, the issue of offense will be related to God's leadership and the release of God's judgment activities (or relative lack of action): *Why did God intervene on behalf of that other guy when I did the exact same thing and nothing happened?*

Scripture warns that at the end of the age there will be great tribulation: Human sin will ripen fully, as prophesied by Jesus in Matthew 13. Meanwhile, satan will be raging in desperation because his time is short

(Revelation 12:12-17). In addition, creation's groan will be fully released resulting in natural and geological upheaval. Finally, God will release his temporal judgments against the gods of the earth like in the days of Moses and the Exodus to set free people from delusion and rescue them from the ultimate consequences of sin.

The invitation open to you:

With all of the confusion and pain associated with injustice at end of the age, how can the Body of Christ stay confident in the goodness of God? Thankfully, the Bride of Christ will not be left without wisdom and understanding. Jeremiah prophesied of God's people in those days:

See, the storm of the LORD will burst out in wrath, a driving wind swirling down on the heads of the wicked. The fierce anger of the LORD will not turn back until he fully accomplishes the purposes of his heart. In days to come you will understand this. (Jeremiah 30:23-24)

The prophet Daniel also wrote of a people who would understand the justice and the judgments of God amidst a generation in crisis:

He replied, "Go your way, Daniel, because the words are closed up and sealed until the time of the end. Many will be purified, made spotless and refined, but the wicked will continue to be wicked. None of the wicked will understand but those who are wise will understand. (Daniel 12:9-10).

As we approach the hour of his return, God promised to raise up a people of understanding.

As we seek to gain understanding, we need to acknowledge our deep need for more wisdom and revelation through the Holy Spirit. Extra-biblical and modern stories may be presented to highlight what is found in the scriptures. While historical stories may be presented as examples of God's justice in action, we must always go back to what the scriptures say.

Around every corner are traps of vain conceit and selfish ambition leading bitterness and offense. History is littered with wrong understanding of God's wisdom and ways. The fruit of no understanding is often very destructive and ruins lives. People perish because of lack of understanding.

God has promised a generation the Key of David (Isaiah 22:22) to open doors that no one can shut. Perhaps this generation has been granted the open door in heaven (Revelation 4:1) to understand what must soon take place. God promised a generation that would have this godly boast:

This is what the LORD says: "Let not the wise man boast of his wisdom or the strong man boast of his strength or the rich man boast of his riches, but let him who boasts boast about this: that he understands and knows me, that I am the LORD, who exercises kindness, justice and righteousness on earth, for in these I delight. (Jeremiah 9:23-24)

Knowing God goes far beyond simply knowing theology, biblical passages, or even how to operate in power and authority. The children of Israel knew God's power in very personal ways. However, only Moses and a few others went behind the veil to understand God's emotions behind the displays of power and majesty. Through the finished work on the cross, the door is open.

In understanding our great need for God's wisdom, we begin our exploration and dialogue to understand the heart of the judge. Only those who seek to know the heartbeat of his emotions can understand deeply. The door is open to know the deep emotions that are hidden in His heart. Justice must begin at the heart. Through looking at the scriptures along with our own hearts, the invitation is open for you to understand Jesus the judge.

Discussion questions:

1. How would you define "justice"?

2. When you hear the term "judgment of God", what is the first thing that comes to mind?

3. If eternal judgment is a foundational doctrine in the Church, why do you think the Church teaches so little on it?

4. Do you think it is possible to understand God's judgments? Why or Why not?

Chapter 2:

Who is Jesus the Judge?

"Jesus the Judge is moving everything that hinders love, moving it out of the way so that love can dominate the created order to those who say 'yes' to Him."- Mike Bickle

"Swindler Sam," said Caring Christian. "I want you to meet my friend, Wise Willie. He has been a trusted advisor and buddy for many years."

"Good to meet you, Wise Willie", said Swindler Sam as he heartily offered his hand. "Would you like to get in on the latest deal I am offering my friend, Caring Christian?"

"No, thank you," said Wise Willie, who suddenly had a concerned look.

"What's the matter, Wise Willie?" replied Caring Christian. "He's offering me a huge investment opportunity. The Mischievous Marketing company has made a few million dollars, and Swindler Sam is offering me equal partnership for $50,000. It's a once-in-a-lifetime opportunity."

"I need to be on to the next business deal. I'll let you talk," said Swindler Sam.

After Swindler Sam left, Wise Willie wasted no time in voicing his concerns.

"I'm concerned," said Wise Willie. "Swindler Sam is doing business in ways that are clearly forbidden in God's Word. He's practicing divination by consulting mediums. Other people who have done business with him have been left with empty wallets and have tried to bring that man to justice. Yet, every time they go after him, Swindler Sam escapes their grasp as they cannot prove their case. Besides, the Bible warns us not to be yoked with unbelievers."

"I'm willing to take the risk," said Caring Christian, raising his voice. "I still don't see the judgment of God against this guy."

"I really care for you and I'm concerned," said Wise Willie quietly. "Remember that God is just and true in all of his ways. You also need to know that God really loves you and is deeply zealous for your overall well-being. However, you must understand that God is also looking out for your future from an eternal perspective."

Who do you say I am?

Like in the days of Jesus, our culture has many different views of who Jesus is. Jesus asked this question to his disciples in Matthew 16, and this is the question that he asks of us today:

"Who do people say that the Son of Man is?" (Matthew 16:13)

Just as in the days of Jesus, those claiming to be the people of God have different answers! Some say that Jesus simply a historical figure. Others say that he is a fraud. Still others hold him to be a teacher. Yet another group says that he is simply a prophet (not *THE Prophet*). Who is Jesus? Our eternal destiny depends on the answer to this question.

Following the narrative in Matthew 16 we find Peter comes up with the correct answer to the quiz. Jesus affirms Peter's answer:

Jesus replied, "Blessed are you, Simon son of Jonah, for this was not revealed to you by man, but by my Father in heaven. And I tell you that you are Peter, and on this rock I will build my church, and the gates of Hades will not overcome it. I will give you the keys of the kingdom of heaven; whatever you bind on earth will be bound in heaven, and whatever you loose on earth will be loosed in heaven." (Matthew 16:17-19)

It doesn't matter what satan or his minions do, or what evil men do- Jesus is still Lord. The worldly systems, creation's groan, and humanity's sin will not stop God. Upon the revelation of Jesus Christ, God will build his church and his kingdom.

Meanwhile, Peter has just received one of the greatest affirmations of anyone in all of scripture. He had to be ecstatic! According to popular belief, if Jesus is the Son of God, it means that Jesus will rule and that Peter and his buddies get to rule the world with Jesus. Instead of getting stomped on by foreign powers (and peers), Peter and his friends get to do the stomping. Unperceived, self-conceit mixed with the euphoria was filling Peter's head, causing his ego to expand like an over grown hot-air balloon.

Of course, Jesus began to talk about the suffering and death (not to mention resurrection) he would need to go through as the Son of Man. Filled with euphoria-induced ego, Peter decided to "intervene":

Peter took him aside and began to rebuke him. "Never, Lord!" he said. "This shall never happen to you!" (Matthew 16:22)

Suffering and death could never happen to the Messiah. In popular Jewish culture, the Messiah was to be a warrior who would kill off all the bad gentile nations and rule over the whole earth with the Jewish people especially favored. Besides, Peter's position and the honor of world leadership over others needed to be defended.

Unfortunately or fortunately, the word of God is compared to a double-edged sword. When something sharp like the Word Incarnate pierces a ballooning ego, something painful and explosive happens:

Jesus turned and said to Peter, "Get behind me, Satan! You are a stumbling block to me; you do not have in mind the things of God, but the things of men." (Matthew 16:23)

Jesus followed one of the highest affirmations of a man with one of the most severe rebukes in all of scripture. Peter's dream (or delusion) of stomping those evil nations and lording it over everyone was left in shambles. Poor Peter went from the heights of euphoria down to the depths of humiliation and despair, all within a matter of a few verses!

So what does this tell us about Jesus? First, it shows that Jesus Christ is deeply interactive and relational. Our understanding of Jesus the Judge must comes in a relational context. Second, it also shows Jesus' willingness as a judge to affirm what is right and violently oppose what is bad-even if it really creates difficulties and pain. Third, it tells us that Jesus is deeply settled in his identity and mission. No one will stop him from being loyal to his Father.

How can God grow in favor with God?

The scriptures clearly indicate that Jesus knew who he was, even as a newly bar mitzvah-ed man. We call Jesus the Son of God, the Son of Man, Savior, Master, King of kings, Lord of lords and glorious. He is the Kinsman redeemer, the Lion of the Tribe of Judah, The Prophet of Deuteronomy 18, the Chief Shepherd, and the Lord of the Armies. Jesus is the Key of David, and the Desire of the Nations. Immediately, his parents found Jesus busy about his Father's business.

Luke 2:52 is a very troubling verse to many orthodox Christian theologians. Jesus had just been found by his parents in dialogue with the rabbis about the scriptures. Even at a very young age, he was involved in his Father's business as a carpenter. As a summary statement regarding his youth, the scripture says:

And Jesus grew in wisdom and stature, and in favor with God and men. (Luke 2:52)

The troubling question is: *If Jesus is completely God from birth, how can he grow in favor with God and man?* If Jesus needs to grow in favor with God, does it mean that Jesus was anything less than God at some point? Does it validate process theology where God is still becoming God? Is it possible that the scripture made an error here making it fallible? All of these can raise troubling points to our trust in God.

Instead of contradicting itself, the Bible was describing fellowship of absolute beauty and astonishment within God. Jesus had absolute favor with the Father from eternity past. Let's say that Jesus grew in one unit of favor due to the temple incident. Jesus still had absolute favor with God as absolute infinity of favor plus one unit of favor (or even an absolute infinite number of units of favor) is still absolute infinity. It is our finite human minds that need to count units of favor as we do not understand the infinite or eternal.

Yet the scripture says that Jesus grew in favor with God. Jesus was surely worshiping the Father in the temple in obedience to the Mosaic law. How can Jesus grow in favor with God through worshipping him if he is God? If Jesus has all the favor, how can he grow in favor with God? This doesn't make sense unless we are stumbling upon a hidden, shocking, beautiful, and unchanging attribute of the Most High God: The Father, Son, and the Holy Spirit have been growing in favor, honor, and righteousness relationally from eternity past.

While Jesus has been growing in favor with the Father and the Spirit, Jesus never changed his character and nature. The righteousness of God has unfolded from eternity past. David said of Jesus in visions:

Righteousness and justice are the foundation of your throne; love and faithfulness go before you. Blessed are those who have learned to acclaim you, who walk in the light of your presence, O LORD. They rejoice in your name all day long; they exult in your righteousness. (Psalm 89:14-16)

Your throne, O God, will last forever and ever; a scepter of justice will be the scepter of your kingdom. You love righteousness and hate wickedness; therefore God, your God has set you above your companions by anointing you with the oil of joy. (Psalm 45:6-7)

Eternity past unfolded as Father, Son, and Holy Spirit walked in radiant righteousness. Now the only difference was that Jesus walked on the earth. Many years earlier, God had formed Adam and Eve in his image. Now God the Creator was walking the earth in the likeness of men. Nothing had changed in terms of his delight in righteousness and a hatred of wickedness. The beauty of God's eternal righteousness is revealed through how the Father, Son, and Holy Spirit interact with each other in a pivotal moment on earth: the baptism of Jesus.

Divine honor and joy at the baptism of Jesus

In Luke, we find that even in the womb, John the Baptist prophesied the coming of Jesus. Mary had an angelic visitation and realized that she and Joseph needed to get to Elizabeth's house for refuge. As Elizabeth met Mary, John leaped in Elizabeth's womb, overjoyed in the Holy Spirit.

With the supernatural events surrounding John's birth, Israel was waiting for God to act through this man in the wilderness. Matthew records the events:

In those days John the Baptist came, preaching in the Desert of Judea and saying, "Repent, for the kingdom of heaven is near." This is he who was spoken of through the prophet Isaiah: "A voice of one calling in the desert, 'Prepare the way for the Lord, make straight paths for him.' "(Matthew 3:1-3)

After over 400 years of silence, the prophetic word of the Lord broke in through John the Baptist. Drawn by the power of the Holy Spirit, multitudes of people came out to listen to this firebrand preacher in the wilderness.

Thousands of people, pricked to the core by John's message, confessed their sins and repented. To demonstrate their repentance, they submitted to water baptism. Filled with the fire of God, John warned the self-righteous religious leaders:

"I baptize you with water for repentance. But after me will come one who is more powerful than I, whose sandals I am not fit to carry. He will baptize you with the Holy Spirit and with fire. His winnowing fork is in his hand, and he will clear his threshing floor, gathering his wheat into the barn and burning up the chaff with unquenchable fire." (Matthew 3:11-12)

With this renewal of Messianic passion, John got a surprise. Jesus Christ, whom all of his prophecy was pointing to, walked up to John and wanted to be baptized.

Why did he want to be baptized? John saw that he is the one to baptize with the Holy Spirit and fire. Why was Jesus coming here? Staggered at who was in front of him and overwhelmed over his sudden need to be cleansed, Matthew 3:14 tells us:

John tried to deter him, saying, "I need to be baptized by you, and do you come to me?" Jesus replied, "Let it be so now; it is proper for us to do this to fulfill all righteousness." Then John consented. (Matthew 3:14-15)

Why was Jesus Christ, God almighty in the flesh, submitting to a mere mortal?

What we don't see in the narrative is the one who was upon John. Jesus wasn't only submitting to John, he was submitting to the Holy Spirit upon John. John as a friend of the Bridegroom was the honored vessel. God the Son was serving and honoring the Holy Spirit. This after God the Holy Spirit honored and glorified God the Son by pointing him out to the amazement of onlookers (along with Mary and Elizabeth so many years earlier). Matthew 3:16 describe what happens next:

As soon as Jesus was baptized, he went up out of the water. At that moment heaven was opened, and he saw the Spirit of God descending like a dove and lighting on him. (Matthew 3:16)

Not to take the glory and honor, the Holy Spirit quickly presented Jesus before the crowd. God the Holy Spirit came upon the Jesus as a dove coming from heaven.

Not to be outdone by the divine pleasure and joy taking place on earth, heaven opened and God the Father joined in:

And a voice from heaven said, "This is my Son, whom I love; with him I am well pleased." (Matthew 3:17)

In submitting to baptism of repentance, Jesus honored the Father and his will. For the first time since he thundered the Ten Commandments, the world heard the audible voice of God as the Father gave his thunderous approval of Jesus before all of Israel.

The humble God who kneels

The Divine drama around the baptism of Jesus gives a sample of what has been happening between Father, Son, and Holy Spirit from all of eternity. Jesus, the exact representation of the Father, was making known what God was like in his humility and righteousness. Jesus would later express the fullness of that love in the heart of Father, Son, and Holy Spirit. The beauty and righteousness of God was openly displayed that day, and the nations trembled.

Throughout history, God showed mercy to people who had done really disgusting things. Jacob manipulated Esau into selling his birthright. David slept with Uriah's wife Bathsheba and then politically maneuvered his team to get Uriah killed. Manasseh filled Jerusalem with bloodshed. Jesus transformed the woman at the well in John 4. Jesus ate at Zacchaeus's house, a hated tax collector who swindled everyone. Yet in every case, God had mercy on them because they humbled themselves before him.

In contrast, God put Joseph into slavery for years simply because he bragged about his prophetic promises to his brothers. God dealt with Israel and David harshly because David numbered the fighting men of Israel. As the result of this haughty act, 70,000 men died. This was far greater than the number killed in a civil war initiated by Absalom as part of the judgment from the ordeal with Bathsheba.

Solomon's pride led to destruction. Solomon started out his kingship brilliantly by asking for wisdom from God. God favored the humility behind Solomon's request and gave Solomon everything which led to conceit.

After everything God had done for him, he turned to other gods and became like Saul. In the pride of his latter years, Solomon attempted to kill a future king of the northern tribes.

God struck Uzziah with leprosy after he became proud and went into the temple and burned unauthorized incense there. Jesus rebuked the religious leaders because of their unbridled arrogance and oppression. Later, Herod was eaten by worms because in his arrogance, he opposed God and did not give glory to the King of Heaven.

It is clear from these numerous examples that God deeply values meekness and humility while he absolutely hates pride.

To fear the LORD is to hate evil; I hate pride and arrogance, evil behavior and perverse speech. (Proverbs 8:13)

"Heaven is my throne, and the earth is my footstool. Where is the house you will build for me? Where will my resting place be? Has not my hand made all these things and so they came into being?" declares the LORD. "This is the one I esteem: he who is humble and contrite in spirit, and trembles at my word. (Isaiah 66:1-2)

From a mere human perspective, it appears that Jesus the judge over reacted to human pride and under reacted to other disgusting vile acts such as conspiracy to murder, financial impropriety, and sexual immorality. Why the apparent disparity?

When God chose Abraham in Genesis 12, God spoke of his role to bring blessing to the nations. In other words, it was not about Abraham; it was about the nations God loves. Jesus as the fulfillment of that prophecy said of himself:

Take my yoke upon you and learn from me, for I am gentle and humble in heart, and you will find rest for your souls. (Matthew 11:29)

Jesus self described himself as meek and humble in heart.

Meanwhile, Isaiah 14 and Ezekiel 28 describe Lucifer, who was once anointed by God and selfishly exalted himself against God. Lucifer became an adversary to God, bringing untold sorrow in heaven. This first sin brought untold destruction and pain to the created order-the celestial root of injustice.

The God who created us was the same God who in John 13 knelt before His disciples. Jesus took up the towel to wash their feet -the job of the least favored slave. After cleansing off the manure and cleaning any sores, Jesus told his astonished disciples:

"You call me 'Teacher' and 'Lord', and rightly so for that is what I am. Now that I, your Lord and Teacher have washed your feet, you also should wash one another's feet." (John 13:13-14)

In the midst of perfect righteousness and purity, God incarnate washed the disciples' feet to show the heart posture of the Father, Son, and Holy Spirit towards each other. Arrogance and pride are the antithesis of the very nature of God's heart and communion. Meanwhile the baptism of Jesus gives us understanding of the unending reservoir of joy and honor within the Trinitarian God.

Divine beauty, righteousness, and chaotic order

Growing up in Minnesota, I used to both fear and love big storms. I wanted to experience the big storm (not really understanding that "big storms" can do "big damage"). On the big day, the air grew calm and heavy. The sky changed from a shrouded blue and white to a menacing dark color with a hint of green. Meanwhile, a distant thunder rolled and lightning flashed. The blaring sirens signaled something big and dangerous was approaching. Like a tympani roll in the concert hall, the thunder occasionally rolls, signaling the beginning of the main event.

Suddenly the calm and relative silence broke as the first winds whistled through the trees. The first drops of rain spanked the roof. Within less than a minute, leaves were now flying through the air as trees were bent over. The first drops of rain turned into blinding sheets combined with chunks of ice. The din of thunder, wind, rain, and hail on the roof was only interrupted with an explosive crash as lightning struck a bit too close for comfort. I found beauty in the midst of the chaos.

The storms on the earth pale in comparison with the terror and beauty found in the storm of heaven: Scripture passages such as Isaiah 6:1-6, Daniel 7:1-6, Ezekiel 1, and Revelation 4-5 give tremendous insight into the terrifying majesty and beauty of God. Beautifully complex and apparently chaotic, yet with absolute purpose and order, God issues forth his righteous decrees.

Various prophetic men have seen lightning, fire, an emerald rainbow, a sea of glass, streets made of gold, precious stones, treasures, and feasting. They have also heard thunder, voices, trumpets, other musical instruments, heavenly shouts, other voices, and the roar of multitudes worshiping God in celebration and joy. Undoubtedly, some felt the winds of God, as Jesus compared the movements of the Holy Spirit to wind. Men like John and Isaiah fell flat on their faces upon encountering the storm of beauty related to God's holiness.

King David is called as man after God's own heart. Under his leadership, the Ark of the Covenant, a symbol of God's glory, was openly seen before the nations of the earth. David got glimpses of God's beauty which only fueled a desire to see more:

One thing I ask of the LORD, this is what I seek: that I may dwell in the house of the LORD all the days of my life, to gaze upon the beauty of the LORD and to seek him in his temple. (Psalm 27:4)

Splendor and majesty are before him; strength and glory are in his sanctuary. Ascribe to the LORD, O families of nations, ascribe to the LORD glory and strength. Ascribe to the LORD the glory due his name; bring an offering and come into his courts. Worship the LORD in the splendor of his holiness; tremble before him all the earth. (Psalm 96:6-9)

Moses cried out to see the glory of God, and God granted his request within strict limits. What Moses saw caused him to fall flat on his face in worship.

In declaring the beauty and majesty of God, Jesus gave further insight into this glorious communion when he said:

"I tell you the truth, the Son can do nothing by himself; he can do only what he sees his Father doing, because whatever the Father does the Son also does. For the Father loves the Son and shows him all he does. Yes, to your amazement he will show him even greater things than these."(John 5:19-20)

This is the man, eternally begotten of the Father, who participated in creation described in Genesis 1. God created as the Word was released from the Father and the Spirit, hovering over creation, acted. Beginning with light, the heavens and the earth came forth.

Beholding the spectacle of creation was a royal angelic court full of majesty and honor. God spoke of this beauty and majesty before a stricken man filled with confusion over his circumstances:

Where were you when I laid the earth's foundation? Tell me, if you understand. Who marked off its dimensions? Surely you know! Who stretched a measuring line across it? On what were its footings set, or who laid its cornerstone-while the morning stars sang together and all the angels shouted for joy? (Job 38:4-7)

Out of the beauty and majesty of God, the earth and the heavens came forth in their entire righteous splendor. Since the fall, even the most glorious sunset and even the most majestic mountain peak is but a faint image of the beauty and majesty of his righteousness. This is the same God who kneels in meekness out of the reservoir of joy in the midst of fellowship in Father, Son, and Holy Spirit.

"I the Lord your God am a Jealous God"

This eternal storm of beauty and righteous majesty came within sight of the earth. Imagine standing before a tall mountain- except that you cannot see the very top of the mountain. There is darkness all around as the clouds blot out the sun and the stars. The darkness is punctuated with sizzling white lightning and an ominous fire burning, consuming, hidden within the clouds of darkness and billowing smoke on top of the mountain. There is no way to retreat, nowhere to run, nowhere to hide.

In the midst of the terrifying sight are terrifying sounds of trumpets, voices, and thunder. The thunder appears to have many voices in it- awesome and thunderous like the sound of a Niagara Falls or the surf smashing upon the rocks during a violent gale. Suddenly in the midst of this awesome and terrifying sight, a tender, rich, firm, ear-splitting voice sounding like a lion roaring thunders from the top of the mountain.

As you have probably guessed, I am describing the scene from Exodus 19 that a young, newly liberated Hebrew slave may have experienced. Grateful after the Red Sea, yet confused with the new diet plan, the question on everyone's mind: *Who is this "hidden" God that Abraham knew as his exceedingly great reward?*

Hebrews 12 tells us that even Moses trembled with fear at the sight of the one who is an all-consuming fire. No wonder why Moses had warned them not to go near that mountain! In the midst of trembling, the fire, and the quaking mountain, the God of Abraham, Isaac, and Jacob was communicating something far deeper than what mere words can fully express- his holy jealousy over us. Jeremiah would later call this Mount Sinai moment a betrothal ceremony.

Our understanding of God's life-giving jealousy is in sharp contrast with human jealousy and bitter envy. Bitter envy is the human desire for something that is not ours. James addressed the sin of bitter envy:

What causes fights and quarrels among you? Don't they come from your desires that battle within you?

You want something but don't get it. You kill and covet, but you cannot have what you want. You quarrel and fight. You do not have because you do not ask God. When you ask, you do not receive, because you ask with wrong motives, that you may spend what you get on your pleasures. (James 4:1-3)

Bitter envy is the source of much division and strife within the Body of Christ. It is behind murmuring, grumbling, and complaining.

Worse than bitter envy is human self-centered jealousy that leads to jealous rage. Jealousy is all about desiring things that rightfully and exclusively belong to us. Most of our human jealousy is based upon presumption. The problem with human jealousy is that we presume we have a right to much more than what the Bible specifically declares is rightfully ours. We presume that our bodies, our material resources, our relationships, our specific role or job, our gifts, and talents all belong to us. We actually own nothing but are stewards of the things that God has graciously given to us.

Self-centered, human jealousy adds an entitlement dimension to bitter envy, making it almost impossible to break. In the case of Cain, he would not even listen to the counsel of God on the matter. His self-centered jealousy led to hatred and then the murder of his brother Abel. Many kingdom of God initiatives have been destroyed through bitter envy and human jealousy that led to strife.

The Bible gives only a few examples of human jealousy being righteous through covenant: It is right for a bridegroom to jealously defend his bride against others who would intimately use her because of God's prohibition against adultery. It is right for God's people to jealously desire the LORD our God. Our God, as the creator and sustainer of the universe rightly desires us for his purposes because we are his creation. The apostle Paul described himself as jealous for his disciples with a godly jealousy.

God reveals himself as Jealous- but what is the dream for humanity behind his burning jealousy? God gave insight into what is on his heart after a generation committed themselves, their children, and their children's children for every generation to fear and obey God:

"I have heard what this people said to you. Everything the said was good. Oh, that their hearts would be inclined to fear me and keep all my commands always, so that it might go well with them and their children forever!" (Deuteronomy 5:28-29).

God's jealousy is unlike, our selfish-centered jealousy and bitter envy that sulks when we don't get our way. God did not give instructions to oppress people or to make them perform. God's counsel was to set them free to have the fullness of joy, righteousness, and prosperity.

Before sin entered the picture, God breathed on humanity and created him in the image of God which included eternal existence. Designed to live forever in the presence of God, Adam walked with God. Before sin and associated death entered the human experience, Adam enjoyed unrestrained joy and fellowship with God. God gave specific instructions to Adam so that he could enjoy communion with God to the fullest.

The sin of Adam and Eve did not change God's eternal nature. Even after sin entered the picture, God wants us to enjoy as much fellowship with him as possible. God gave instructions to his people for the sake of enjoying fellowship with him and each other. Indeed, God's jealousy burns with a self-sacrificing fire that is desirous for our relational, emotional, and physical well-being forever.

The greatest commandment, the greatest promise

After washing the disciples' feet, Jesus inaugurated the new covenant with bread and wine. In the midst of taking the bread and the cup, Jesus gave thanks. Jesus showed them the full extent of his love and humility.

Before feeding the 5,000 Jesus gave thanks for the five loaves and two fishes. Before them was standing God incarnate, who *created* the bread and the fish with the Father and the Spirit before time began, giving thanks. Has

44

anyone considered what this means about God and what we are invited into?

If Jesus gave thanks and honor to his Father, surely it means we can also give thanks and praise for the good things he has done, and enter into fellowship with God. Even Psalm 22 (which Jesus quoted part of on the darkest day of history) ends with praise and honor to God. God even commanded it:

When you have eaten and are satisfied, praise the LORD your God for the good land he has given you. Be careful that you do not forget the LORD your God, failing to observe his commands, his laws and his decrees that I am giving you this day. (Deuteronomy 8:10-11)

In the midst of his decree, God was commanding us to give thanks. Gratitude and honor of others was a sign of walking in deep humility. With this command was the invitation to join the fellowship of Father, Son, and Holy Spirit where there are pleasures forevermore.

In an attempted to trap Jesus, the religious leaders asked him what the greatest commandment is. Jesus ended his recorded public ministry with an emphatic response:

"The most important one", answered Jesus, "is this: 'Hear O Israel, the Lord our God, the Lord is one. Love the Lord your God with all your heart and with all your soul and with all your mind and with all your strength.' The second is this: 'Love your neighbor as yourself.' There is no commandment greater than these." (Mark 12:29-31)

There is far more than meets the eye related to this commandment. There are many reason why this is truly the greatest commandment. I will limit it to five:

First, the one who commanded this is the greatest: God is superior in passion, wisdom, knowledge, power, authority, and riches. Above the kings of the earth and every other human authority, in all things Jesus is preeminent and superior. God is asking us to love him with everything *because this is the way he loves us.*

Second, the greatest commandment comes with the greatest difficulty to obey consistently. Life in this age is filled with distractions, difficulties, perplexity, and pain. Can we fully obey this commandment in the mundane routine of normal life, in the midst of great difficulty, persecution, or great prosperity?

Third, hidden within the greatest commandment is access to the greatest power. In order to command mere humans to do something, there must be the grace (power) available to do it. Apart from God, no one can do anything. Yet with the Holy Spirit, anything is possible. Jesus was filled with the Holy Spirit without measure while totally dependent upon the anointing of the Holy Spirit.

Forth, failure to obey the greatest commandment brings the greatest negative consequences. Sin began with the choice to not love God first in favor of sin. The growth of sin leading to judgment and wrath is ultimately because of the failure to obey the greatest commandment.

Fifth, the greatest commandment brings the greatest eternal reward and joy. This is the way God loves us and desires good for us. In giving us the greatest commandment, God commands us to come to the place of communion with him, the place of eternal power, glory, and pleasure.

God burns with jealous desire for our eternal glory. God the Father desires sons who would rule with him in the beauty of righteousness, joy, and peace. Jesus as a Bridegroom desires a Bride who knows the deep things that are on his heart. At the very end, the Bride is clothed like Jesus in garments of radiant righteousness, sounds like Jesus with the voice of many waters, and acts like Jesus. Meanwhile, the Holy Spirit desires a resting place in humanity where he is unhindered to act in displaying the awesome works of God. Within the burning, jealous heart of God is his invitation to join in on the divine, unending fellowship of righteousness, joy, peace, and unending pleasure.

This was the dream of God for humanity before the foundation of the world, that we would experience the glories and pleasures of God forever with our children. At his right hand are pleasures forevermore which he desires to share with us. Our God is zealous for our well-being forever.

Discussion questions:

1. Describe a "God encounter" that you have had in life. What did God show you about himself?

2. Why is understanding the identity and attributes of God so important?

3. How does God want to interact with us, and why is this important?

Chapter 3:

The wrath of the Judge

"I shall tell you a great secret my friend. Do not wait for the last judgment, it takes place every day."- Albert Cumus

"What?" said Caring Christian. "God, I can't believe it!"

"What's the problem?" said Wise Willy.

"My business partner, Swindler Sam, swindled me out of $50,000 and got me canned from the company. Now I just read in our local paper that Swindler Sam got the Earthly Entrepreneur award for 'Shrewd Businessman of the Year' along with a $1,000,000 bonus" whined Caring Christian.

"Why did you get involved with Swindler Sam?" asked Wise Willy. "You knew that Swindler Sam is clearly not following Jesus, but you love Jesus with all your heart. You know what the Bible says about not being unequally yoked when trust is critical in the relationship. Maybe God cares about you so much that he intervened before you learned Swindler Sam's ways."

Caring Christian continued: "Swindler Sam cheats on everyone through his smooth lips and deception. Yet his family is doing well, he is in good health, and doing well economically. Meanwhile, my family is a wreck, and we are now barely making ends meet. Where is the justice of God in this?"

"Have you ever considered that Swindler Sam may be under the wrath of God?" asked Wise Willy.

"If Swindler Sam is under 'the wrath of God', I need some of that 'wrath of God' for my family!" retorted Caring Christian.

Caring Christian's reaction represents the pain many true followers of Jesus in America and in the nations of the earth are currently suffering. God seems to lets fake Christians and pagan unbelievers get away with pretty much anything they want to do. As the result, they "run amok" and do some rather disgusting things and then appear to get away with it before God. Meanwhile, the same actions done by God's beloved ones bring swift discipline from God, sorrow, and pain. Why?

Beginning in September 2008, God shook America's economy along with the nations of the world. Stock prices declined at an alarming rate as iconic American businesses went under. This propelled America into what many have dubbed, "The Great Recession". The average household family income dropped roughly 10%.

However, the impact was far more severe upon charities in general, and more specifically the Church. Charitable contributions dropped more than 50%, giving American Christians a portrait of where our hearts are truly at. Thousands of congregations permanently closed their doors in the midst of the financial pressure. While God was shaking the world's economic systems, the discipline upon the Body of Christ was far more intense- why?

Where is the justice of God in situations like this? Countless prophets and theologians have wrestled with this issue. The prosperity of the wicked juxtaposed with the suffering of the righteous has perplexed many. Jacob figuratively and literally wrestled with God while Esau lived on easy street under Isaac's tent. Habakkuk wrestled with this issue as Babylon was closing in on Jerusalem. Why was God disciplining Israel by using an empire that was far more idolatrous, ruthless, and evil? To make things worse, why was God going even further and apparently blessing Israel's disciplinarians?

Perhaps the greatest theologian at the heart level was David. David was hiding in caves while Saul was resting comfortably in the palace. Saul had sent out 3,000 of Israel's finest to capture and kill him. Out of his wrestling and pain he wrote,

Surely, God is good to Israel, to those who are pure in heart. But as for me, my feet had almost slipped; I had nearly lost my foothold. For I envied the arrogant when I saw the prosperity of the wicked. They have no struggles; their bodies are healthy and strong. They are free from the burdens common to man; they are not plagued by human ills. (Psalm 73:1-5)

In this case, David's offended mind and difficult circumstances were proving something extremely precious to God. Many people when faced with situations like this end up turning away from God. Yet David continued to wait and proved that he was a man after God's own heart.

How can someone be greatly prosperous, yet be under the wrath of God? It appears to be an oxymoron in scripture. The cultural norm in a materialistic culture without the fear of God says: Obedience brings material blessing, disobedience brings poverty. While sounding good, it points to a bigger problem in society. As discussed in the opening chapter, our society and much of the Body of Christ is still in early childhood or infancy in terms of understanding the judgments of God.

Understanding the anger of a broken heart:

In American Christianity, wealth is viewed as generally a sign of God's blessing while poverty is generally a sign of God's disapproval. Yet, wealth does not always mean God's blessing is upon a person. Meanwhile, poverty does not always mean that God is displeased with someone.

Indeed, scripture gives plenty of examples of people who were not experiencing wealth, comfort, or ease and yet God was pleased with them. Scripture also gives plenty of examples of people who were experiencing wealth, riches, and honor on earth and yet they were under the wrath of God. Moses prophesied about Israel's prosperity and how an arrogant, ungrateful, idolatrous response would bring God's anger:

Jeshurun grew fat and kicked; filled with food he became heavy and sleek. He abandoned the God who made him and rejected the Rock his Savior. They made him jealous with their foreign gods and angered him with their detestable idols. They sacrificed to demons, which are not God-gods they had not known, gods that recently appeared, gods your fathers did not fear. You deserted the Rock, who fathered you; you forgot the God who gave you birth.

The Lord saw this and rejected them because he was angered by his sons and daughters. "I will hide my face

53

from them," he said, "and see what their end will be; for they are a perverse generation, children who are unfaithful. They made me jealous by what is no god and angered me with their worthless idols."
(Deuteronomy 32:15-21)

The people were still experiencing wealth and honor from the world. Yet, because they had departed from following the LORD, God was angry at them.

The issue was more than simply failing to obey a set of rules and precepts. God wanted a relationship that went beyond simply following instructions:

The wrath of God is being revealed from heaven against all the godlessness and wickedness of men who suppress the truth by their wickedness, since what may be known about God is plain to them because God has made it plain to them. For since the creation of the world God's invisible qualities-his eternal power and divine nature-have been clearly seen, being understood from what has been made, so that men are without excuse.

For although they knew God, they neither glorified him as God nor gave thanks to him, but their thinking became futile and their foolish hearts were darkened. Although they claimed to be wise, they became fools and exchanged the glory of the immortal God for images made to look like mortal men and birds and animals and reptiles. (Romans 1:18-23)

In giving the Torah, God was giving Israel a deep invitation beyond the rules and regulations. God wanted something far deeper, far greater:

Hear, O Israel: the LORD our God, the LORD is one. Love the LORD your God with all your heart and with all your soul and with all your strength. (Deuteronomy 6:4-5)

From the last chapter, we understand this great invitation: With the greatest commandment was the greatest invitation to walk in wisdom and understanding leading to the greatest eternal joy and well-being. God revealed his glory before the whole nation and Israel with the cloud by day and the fire by night. The prophet Ezekiel offered God's commentary of those years:

"Later I passed by, and when I looked at you and saw that you were old enough for love, I spread the corner of my garment over you and covered your nakedness. I gave you my solemn oath and entered into a covenant with you," declares the Sovereign LORD, "and you became mine." (Ezekiel 16:8)

God also spoke through the prophet Jeremiah related to those years:

"'I remember the devotion of your youth, how as a bride you loved me and followed me through the desert, through a land not sown. Israel was holy to the LORD, the first fruits of his harvest; all who devoured her were held guilty, and disaster overtook them,'" declares the LORD. (Jeremiah 2:2-3)

God compared those early days to a young man in love with a young woman. Yet, Israel turned away to follow other gods, provoking God to anger.

Unlike God who never changes, people often change our minds. Beginning with Lot's wife, God warned in numerous passages of scripture against turning back to sin and following other gods:

But if a righteous man turns from his righteousness and commits sin and does the same detestable things the wicked man does, will he live? None of the righteous things he has done will be remembered. Because of the unfaithfulness he is guilty of and because of the sins he has committed, he will die. (Ezekiel 18:24)

Judas Iscariot as a disciple of Jesus, did many miracles, proclaimed the kingdom of God, and did many good things. Yet in the end he betrayed Jesus for 30 pieces of silver. What is he most remembered for?

When deeply in love with someone, the only thing they can think of is that special "someone". For example, in 2000, when my sister was dating Chad and preparing for marriage, "Chad" was the only thing she would talk about: Chad this, Chad that. Any conversation was all about marriage with Chad, wise Chad, hanging Chad, swinging Chad, 3-point Chad, 4-point Chad, and even presidential Chad. My sister had "dove's eyes" related to this young man. It did not matter if she had no money- she had Chad. Woe to anything that got in the way of love.

Sadly, I've also sat with both men and women whose wife or husband left them for someone else. Devastated and betrayed, their hearts raged with anger against the one who left them (and often against the God who allowed such a horrible thing to happen). Even secular society recognizes the destruction caused by adultery and betrayal.

The reaction of people (who are imperfect and at least somewhat selfish) is deep fury out of feeling betrayed and scorned. How much greater is God's fury over betrayal and scorned love in the form of sin? Out of jealous desire, God invited people into a place of privilege and glory not even the angels enjoy. God offered us the eternal pleasure and fellowship in relating to Father, Son, and Spirit forever. Far from a passive "no" because of ignorance or misunderstanding, we have collectively responded with a passionate and deliberate "no" through our sinful self-centeredness.

God's offer of righteousness, peace, and joy was an infinite offer. Our deliberate, passionate, "no" constituted an infinite act of treachery that deserved infinite consequences. Scripture clearly says:

For jealousy arouses a husband's fury, and he will show no mercy when he takes revenge. (Proverbs 6:34)

Anger is cruel and fury overwhelming, but who can stand before jealousy? (Proverbs 27:4)

Anger, fury, heartbreak, disappointment, rage- they all describe how God feels about humanity's collective "no" in favor of other gods.

However, words cannot fully express the agonizing pain which rebellious decisions to live out a "no" cause the heart of God. This is the root of human injustice, our unjust treatment of God. Beginning with Adam, God was inviting us into fellowship with a reservoir of eternal joy, peace, and righteousness. Yet we deliberately said "no" and scorned his love.

The experience behind Song of Songs 5:1-8 is an invitation to understand how God feels related to how most of the earth responds to him. God commanded Hosea to marry a harlot (who then rejected him for another cheap thrill) so that he could understand how God felt. God allowed Jeremiah to understand some of this agony because Jeremiah was faithful and then God allowed him to be mistreated. Jeremiah cried out in anger and heartache related to this injustice, towards God. (Jeremiah 15:15-18)

Discerning the outpouring of God's anger:

Contrary to popular belief, God is not easily angered. Jesus the Judge is also our faithful High Priest familiar with our current human condition, brokenness, and suffering. His overall disposition is joy and peace within the fellowship of the Trinity and towards us. God also has a burning desire for his people- to experience far more peace and joy through righteousness than what we are experiencing now.

God is not a half-way God. The Bible confidently declares, that "Jesus loves you"; you can be sure that God loves you *with all of his heart.* It will take all of eternity to full experience the fullness of God's love.

This is why when God is truly angry with someone; they are in really *deep* trouble. When God is angry with someone, he is angry at them *with all of his heart.* Far above our human concepts of time, God's anger only lasts for a moment. However the wicked who angered God, will experience "a moment" of God's anger for all of eternity unless there is repentance.

So out of his anger, what does God do against those who have angered him in the land of the living? Does God throw a tantrum like a spoiled two-year old that didn't get his way? Or is God like those on television who coldly calculate the demise of their adversaries? Popular culture often depicts God as filled with wrathful vengeance against sinners by releasing lightning bolts to strike evil people dead on the spot or sending fire and brimstone upon the wicked in the earth. Often popular belief about God and the biblical texts contradict each other.

Unlike men, God does not hold bitterness or grudges. God's overall disposition of joy and peace within the Trinitarian fellowship is not disrupted. Unmoved by the urgency of the now, God acts to establish righteousness and justice on the earth in perfect wisdom with precise timing displaying his majesty and beauty: If God acted in awesome judgment before with precision, he will do so again. Peter writes:

If this is so, then the LORD knows how to rescue godly men from trials and to hold the unrighteous for the day of judgment, while continuing their punishment. This is especially true of those who follow the corrupt desire of the sinful nature and despise authority.
(2 Peter 2:9-10)

God has all of time and eternity to express his wisdom and righteousness. With pinpoint precision, God can both save the humble and judge the proud simultaneously.

As God's righteous judgments are revealed, Scripture tells the reaction of those present around his throne:

Holy, holy, holy is the LORD Almighty; the whole earth is full of his glory. (Isaiah 6:3)

"In my vision at night I looked, and there before me was one like a son of man, coming with the clouds of heaven. He approached the Ancient of Days and was led into his presence. He was given authority, glory, and sovereign power; all peoples, nations, and men of every language worshiped him. (Daniel 7:13-14)

Whether people choose wickedness or righteousness, the counsel of God stands forever. God's righteousness is unveiled before all. Woe to the wicked as God reveals the beauty of his justice to everyone.

The cruel deception of living under God's wrath

What does God *do* to those who consistently chose rebellion and wickedness against his righteousness? There is no peace for the wicked as they live under the constant threat of eternal judgment. God can surely do or allow anything he wants at anytime to remove them from the earth (and then their eternal fate is sealed) to establish righteousness. No one can stop their appointment with God at the set time.

However, scripture give us some surprising answers of what God does among the living:

I will hide my face from them," he said, "and see what their end will be; for they are a perverse generation, children who are unfaithful." (Deuteronomy 32:20)

God gave them over... (Romans 1:24, 26, 28)

They perish because they refused to love the truth and so be saved. For this reason God sends them a powerful delusion so that they will believe the lie and so that all will be condemned who have not believed the truth but have delighted in wickedness. (2 Thessalonians 2:10-12)

These and other scriptures indicate something surprising to many: God hides his face from the wicked and incrementally gives them over to their sin and the cruel deception of their heart unless they repent.

In other words, God doesn't trouble them-but allows them to go their (often not so) merry way through life in this age while sin and coming eternal retribution increases. Life then has a shocking and very unhappy eternal ending for them. In that day, when they call on God for help, God said that he would not listen.

The first part of this cruel deception those in rebellion face is related to their own immortality. Scripture clearly warns that all will die and then face the judgment (Hebrews 9:27). Few consider how quickly and suddenly man arrives at that final day. Moses said,

You sweep men away in the sleep of death; they are like the new grass of the morning-though in the morning it springs up new, by evening it is dry and withered. (Psalm 90:5-6)

David added:

Show me, O LORD, my life's end and the number of my days; let me know how fleeting is my life. You have made my days a mere handbreadth; the span of my years is as nothing before you. Each man's life is but a breath. (Psalm 39:4-5)

Living in Minnesota and cold climates, there were days in winter when you could literally see your breath. In exhaling out warm, moist air into the cold the water droplets quickly turned into gas that we could briefly see. These small clouds of "breath" are present in one second, gone a second later. Compared to eternity, life on earth in this age is a mere moment.

Furthermore, we also do not know when we will take our last breath on earth. Eternity is a mere breath, one heart-beat away. Ever since the beginning, God has placed a desire to understand eternity into the hearts of people. King Solomon wrote:

I have seen the burden God has laid on men. He has made everything beautiful in its time. He has also set eternity in the hearts of men; yet they cannot fathom what God has done from beginning to end. (Ecclesiastes 3:10-11)

Even some scientists now say that our brains are "hardwired" to believe in God[5]. We all begin with the desire to climb the ladder of success, finish "on top" of the heights of joy and pleasure and for it to last forever. Under deception, the wicked expect to finish "on top" by oppressing others only to find out the bitter truth when it is too late.

The second part of this cruel deception is related to sin- at first, sin appears to be pleasurable as part of the deception. Like a victim who does not know they have cancer, things may appear to go well for them. Sin is like cancer, silently growing often unperceived in the souls of men. Without the sword of God's truth, deception and sin continue to grow. Those under the wrath of God are like victims who have cancer, yet are under strong deception. They will not go to the doctor because of a false belief that the cancer of sin and lawlessness is actually a "good thing" in the name of freedom. When they finally understand the truth, it is too late.

The relatively unrestrained growth of sin

Genesis 3-6 and other passages gave us insight into the destructive growth of sin leading to destruction. In Genesis 3, Adam and Eve disobeyed God by eating from the tree of the knowledge of good and evil. Deceived by the slick serpent, they ate from the tree, believing that selfishness apart from God could give them superior pleasure, joy, and peace over doing things God's way. Gripped with icy shame and the fear of death, they hid from God. Confronted by God, things went downhill when Adam

---

[5] Keller, Mark A. "Brain's reactions to symbols suggest we are hard-wired for God or not. http://national.deseretnews.com/article/2067/brains-reactions-to-symbols-suggest-were-hard-wired-for-god-8212-or-not.html Accessed 8/19/14

blamed Eve (who in turned blamed the snake). The original sin had grown into sinful selfishness at the expense of others cloaked in deceit and blame shifting.

God warned Adam that the day he ate of the tree of the knowledge of good and evil, he would die. Yet, God allowed Adam and Eve and their descendents to physically live for hundreds of years after the disaster in the Garden of Eden. A valid question is *why*? Jonathan Edwards observed:

Sin is the ruin and misery of the soul; it is destructive in its nature; and if God should leave it without restraint, there would need nothing else to make the soul perfectly miserable[6].

There were no instructions against sin-just knowledge that sin had a penalty. In the midst of a nearly perfect physical environment, God gave humanity over to its sin. Genesis 3-6 describes the growth of wickedness and sin without God's active intervention.

Even as Adam and Eve immediately knew that something was wrong after they ate the forbidden fruit, we too know. God has given humanity the gift of conscience in discerning right from wrong. As children, when something was wrong our conscience was pricked. Buried under the deceptive rationalizing ("the means justify the ends") and growing sin, our conscience becomes numb to the deceitfulness and destruction of sin.

As sin grows, relationships further deteriorated. Things got worse with Cain and Abel. Cain as the first born cultivated the fields. This was the "cool job" reminding the family of the original call to be fruitful and multiply. Meanwhile Abel was tending flocks a constant reminder of the penalty for sin. Animals were only used as sacrifices and were not eaten until Genesis 9. Both of them gave offerings.

In a great reversal, the fire of God's approval fell on Abel's offering while God ignored Cain's offering in Genesis 4. Instead of humbling himself before God and Abel, Cain became very angry and bitter at what had just happened.

---

[6] Edwards, Jonathan "Sinners in the hands of an angry God"

Sin had increased from simple selfishness and blame-shifting to outright bitterness and hatred. It was out of bitterness that Cain openly rejected God's counsel and warning.

In rejecting God's counsel, Cain cut himself off from God's grace. Sin then exploded outwardly as he decided to strike Abel down. As Cain was killing Abel, he surely heard his brother's agonizing screams and writhing in pain.

After God confronted Cain, he lied to God's face and then asked a famous (defiant) question:

"I don't know," he replied. "Am I my brother's keeper?" (Genesis 4:9)

In his instructions to Noah and Moses, God shared how he felt about murder and its just punishment. However, God did not immediately put Cain to death physically.

Instead, God judged Cain by saying that he was now under a curse- the earth would no longer produce anything fruitful under his hand. The same hands that had killed would never again bring forth life from the ground. Cain would be forced to stay physically alive by taking from others in fear all the days of his life.

At first this does not seem too bad except that God designed us to live like Jesus to experience the greatest of pleasures. Life in the Kingdom is about blessing, giving, and imparting life to others. It is more blessed to give and serve like Jesus that simply receive and never give out.

In essence, the horrible judgment was that Cain would never produce anything useful to bless and love others again. God did not directly kill Cain but instead left Cain alive for many years to show the terrible consequences of willful sin that would continue to grow in destruction and misery. Under the curse of God and tormented by demons, Cain was in essence a "dead man walking". Cain would never be able to live the way God had intended.

A few generations later, things became even worse. Lamech also killed someone who had wounded him, and then justified his actions before other people. In this way,

Lamech went further by teaching others that it was okay to murder and get revenge. From Lamech's story we learn that people who have been hurt by sin and poisoned by bitterness end up hurting others (often far worse than they were hurt). Like a stream widening into a mighty river, sin and associated bitterness began to increase exponentially on the earth.

Underneath the ever widening river of sin and bitterness is the search for justice. Often justice is confused with vengeance. Vengeance is about "getting even"- something bad happened that needs to be counter-balanced with punishment against the perpetrator. Vengeance can never restore what was made wrong-only true justice can. In the broken hearts of vengeful humanity, true justice is always elusive, just beyond our finger-tips.

By Genesis 6, the earth was filled with bitter cries of wickedness, violence, and hatred. Sin matured on the earth. Humanity was "in bed" with the eternal enemies of God and in deep agreement with them. Scripture records,

The LORD saw how great man's wickedness on the earth had become, and that every inclination of the thoughts of his heart was only evil all the time. The LORD was grieved that he had made man on the earth, and his heart was filled with pain. (Genesis 6:5-6)

Now the earth was corrupt in God's sight and was full of violence. God saw how corrupt the earth had become, for all the people on earth had corrupted their ways. (Genesis 6:11-12)

God had designed humanity to walk with him in the cool of the evening. God had invited men and women to join the circle of fellowship with God the Father, Son, and Holy Spirit in never-ending, always increasing righteousness, joy, and peace. Satan had promised sinful selfishness and unbelief brought superior pleasure. Instead, humanity was filled with the opposite: evil, bitterness, pain, sorrow, and violence that was ever-escalating.

God's justice-all fully get what they "want" and deserve

Imagine what earth would be like if God had not limited humanity's physical lifespan and people lived forever in ever-increasing sin? Beginning with simple selfishness in Genesis 3, sin would have escalated beyond the horror of Genesis 6 into infinite and ultimate suffering. Jonathan Edwards observed:

There is laid in the very nature of carnal men, a foundation for the torments of hell. There are those corrupt principles, in reigning power in them, and in full possession of them, that are seeds of hell fire. These principles are active and powerful, exceeding violent in their nature, and if it were not for the restraining hand of God upon them, they would soon break out, they would flame out after the same manner as the same corruptions, the same enmity does in the hearts of damned souls, and would beget the same torments as they do in them.[7]

By Genesis 6, life on the earth was imitating hell. In order to fulfill the promises in the garden and presevere true humanity, dramatic and devastating intervention was necessary.

Yet some are determined to have their way with sin. Unlike humanity, God is perfectly just and righteous even to the unjust and the wicked. As the expression of the ultimate justice, in deep anger and heartache God gives the wicked exactly what they "wanted" and deserve according to their deeds. The Bible says,

You open your hand and satisfy the desires of every living thing. (Psalm 145:16)

To those who by persistence in doing good seek glory, honor, and immortality, he will give eternal life. But for those who are self-seeking and who reject the truth and follow evil, there will be wrath and anger. There will be trouble and distress for every human being who does evil: first for the Jew, and then for the Gentile; (Romans 2:7-9)

---

[7] Edwards, Jonathan Ibid.

The greatest eternal punishment is that God gives people exactly what they chose on earth along with the full logical consequences of their choices for all eternity.

In their delusion and deception, they didn't realize what they were communicating to God through their sin. Jesus spoke of this coming justice in the Sermon on the Mount.

So in everything, do to others what you would have them do to you, for this sums up the Law and the Prophets. (Matthew 7:12)

By practicing sin against God and other people, they were unknowingly petitioning God to give them the same treatment in full for all eternity. On that horrible last day, which comes suddenly without warning, no one will be able to say God was unjust. God gave them what they "wanted" in perfect recompense-based upon their desires expressed in their actions.

God is bringing together the new heavens and the new earth under the leadership of Jesus. Under his leadership, everyone gets what they "wanted" (or so they thought) based upon their persistent choices. The lake of fire is the geographical location where all can see the final expression of the fullness of sin and the full effects of sin. Of this gruesome spectacle, God spoke through Isaiah:

"And they will go out and look upon the dead bodies of those who rebelled against me; their worm will not die, nor will their fire be quenched, and they will be loathsome to all mankind." (Isaiah 66:24)

People choose to go there through their persistent sinful choices-including rejecting God's solution in Christ Jesus to sin (not realizing the consequences). With great sorrow, God gives them what they "wanted"- the fullness of sin and its escalating consequences expressed in the depths of the lake of fire.

The harvest of sin that lasts forever

Jesus spent more time describe hell and eternal punishment than he did related to eternal life in the kingdom of God. Scripture describes hell as being a place of "outer darkness", "the pit", "a furnace", "where the worm does not die and the fire is not quenched" and a place where "there is weeping and gnashing of teeth". Jesus warned that some would be beaten with "few stripes" (implying less retribution) while others would be beaten with "many stripes" (implying greater retribution from God). In any case, the ultimate end of sin is horrible beyond imagination.

Though they chose against God, God will not be robbed of his glory from their existence. Indeed some scriptures even hint that the Father, Son, and Holy Spirit will enjoy exalting the righteousness of God in the midst of eternal fellowship through executing retribution upon wickedness. The righteousness of God will be exalted even through the unending suffering and torment of wicked angels and men. Scripture clearly tells us:

Therefore God exalted him to the highest place and gave him the name that is above every name, that at the name of Jesus every knee should bow, in heaven and on earth and under the earth, and every tongue confess that Jesus Christ is Lord, to the glory of God the Father. (Philippians 2:9-11)

Indeed, for a brief moment, before evil doers get the fullness of what they had chosen in life, they will have a *brief* experience of what could have been theirs for all of eternity: Every longing and desire met in God. They will briefly know what Jesus offered them through the cross-the love, joy, and peace of being everything they were created for-only to understand the agony of being scorned because of their choices to reject God in favor of their sinful selfishness and arrogance. That one great moment is ultimate reference for eternal regret. *"If only…it could have been eternally different."*

In hell, there is no joy, peace, or any of the attributes of God that we can experience on the earth. There is no comfort, compassion, or righteousness in Hell. There is no life or light either. They had rejected God (either directly or indirectly through clinging to their sin). Therefore God gave them exactly what they "wanted"- an existence outside any type of fellowship with God. Their physical bodies do not work in many ways-they are "dead" in one sense. Yet, they are fully conscious-suffering a living death without end. They rejected making covenant with Jesus Christ, the author of life. Instead, they chose to make a covenant with "death"-dead idols that do not see, hear, or talk. God gave them over to what they had chosen.

Burning to death was among the most horrible ways to die. The United States banned burning at the stake as a form of capital punishment because of its cruelty. Burn injuries were among the most horrible things people can suffer.

I worked with someone who received 3rd degree burns on their legs. He would scream in agony anytime we needed to bathe and treat the wounds. On September 11th 2001, television cameras captured the horror as people jumped from the burning World Trade Center towers. These poor souls reasoned that it would be better to die of "blunt force trauma" (at the end of their fall) rather than face the few seconds of agony by burning to death in the fire and searing heat.

In the lake of fire, the conscious agony of burning in fire never ends. Every nerve in the body collectively screams in searing agony day and night. The taste and smell of acrid smoke, burning sulfur, and rotting flesh never ends. There is nothing that can be done to lessen the pain that is ever-increasing every moment. In choosing actions that directly caused physical pain to others, they were in essence, saying they wanted the same treatment. God obliged and gave them the fullness of what they had "wanted".

Our physical bodies desire things such as rest, food, and water. In the lake of fire, there is no rest or respite from the overwhelming physical and emotional pain.

There is no eating or drinking in hell-only hunger pains and unquenched thirst forever. Money cannot buy relief or a means of escape. The rich man in Luke 16 simply asked for a drop of water to cool his parched tongue. In arrogance, they choose to deprive others of food, water, and other necessities by their actions. Unknowingly, they were communicating their desire to God-according to Matthew 7:12 and God gave it to them-in full.

Jesus warned that the fire is never quenched and the worm never dies. Every longing of the human heart goes unfulfilled forever-eternal hope deferred. Deep unanswered questions of meaning are left to gnaw at the soul of those condemned. Bitter sorrow never ends. Having seen the joy and pleasure that could have been theirs, bitter envy and shame eat at their psyches forever. There is no reconciliation, no mercy, and no peace. There is only bitterness without end mixed with fear and agony as the emotional torment grows without end. Their sin and wickedness caused emotional pain to many-and God gave them their rightful recompense that in ignorance they were asking for through their actions.

In the lake of fire, there is no dignity, honor, or respect. Their names, revered and feared on the earth are now used as a byword and a curse word. None of their social and cultural accomplishments are remembered. Mocked by God and regarded as "foolish" they have been stripped of any honor or dignity they had on the earth, while others enjoy the fruits of their work in fellowship with God. There are no witty "comebacks"-only endless silent shame and embarrassment. They humiliated others and unknowingly petitioned God to do likewise to them. Suffering unending conscious public ostracism and humiliation forever, they are an eternal testimony to sin, the consequences of sin, and the wrath of God poured out in perfect wisdom and righteousness.

Finally, there is no hope in the lake of fire: A few moments of such physical, mental, and emotional anguish are a terrible punishment. God has allowed some to experience the horrors of eternal justice who have come back to tell their story[8]. Even in the worst circumstances on earth, there is always the hope of getting out of it (even by death). Yet the lake of fire is the final expression of the fullness of sin and righteous judgment: Death as an escape "died" in the lake of fire. There is no hope of relief, no hope of physical escape, no hope of ever appealing or overturning the righteous judgment. Like the law of the Medes and Persians, the judgment is final.

Do not be deceived!

Do not be deceived! Sin cannot be compared to simply just a little bit of dirt on otherwise "good humanity". Instead sin is a hideous form of disease imbedded deep in the soul of humanity. Like cancer, it silently grows leading to destruction and death that lasts forever.

God is deeply angry at sin and wickedness- it destroys everything we were meant to experience in God, leading down to utter destruction. God's wrath has been kindled against those who delight in wickedness. Those under God's wrath may even feel safe, but live under the delusion they have chosen for themselves. The psalmist warns:

Surely, you place them on slippery ground; you cast them down to ruin. How suddenly are they destroyed, completely swept away by terrors! (Psalm 73:18-19)

There is a sudden final judgment day. God has to do nothing to bring evil-doers down into eternal judgment. Sin's gravitational pull brings sinners down into perdition except God intervenes. With righteous anger and heartache, God justly gives, to those who rebel and refuse his ways, everything they "want" all the way unto the fullness.

---

[8] I know of multiple people who have experienced a brief taste of the horrors of Hell in spiritual encounters initiated by God. For a few testimonies, go to: http://www.myfathersreputation.com/

If the heart of Jesus the Judge was simply expressed in God's wrath against sin, we would all be in great trouble with no remedy. The Psalmist wrote,

If you, O LORD, kept a record of sins, O Lord, who could stand? But with you there is forgiveness; therefore you are feared. (Psalm 130:3-4)

Thankfully, God's anger against sin is not the end of the story related to understanding the heart of Jesus the judge.

Underneath God's hot displeasure over sin and wickedness, God's heart still burned with a holy jealousy for you and me to enjoy unceasing fellowship with him. The lake of fire was not created for people. Eternal fire was specifically prepared for the devil and his angels who instigated sin which has led to untold amounts of suffering, pain, and sorrow.

God will not let us go "quietly" into the captivity of sin that leads to destruction. Even the betrayal of sin could not stop the furious love of God. With great long-suffering, God waits for people to turn from sin to the source of life. The scripture tells us that God desires no one to be swallowed up in sin and ultimately end up in the lake of fire:

This is good, and pleases God our Savior, who wants all men to be saved and to come to a knowledge of the truth. (1 Timothy 2:3-4)

As we will see in the next few chapters, God as a just judge will not let people slide down the slippery slope of sin that ends in the lake of fire without putting roadblock after roadblock in the way to stop them. Even among those who have chosen to follow Jesus, God releases gentle correction, painful discipline, and even scourging to correct wrong paths. God wants no one to experience the ultimate just consequences we deserve for our sin.

Discussion questions:

1. When you hear the term, "The Wrath of God" what is the first thing that comes to mind?

2. Why do you think God allows people (especially non-believers) to "get away" with wickedness while bringing discipline upon his people for doing the exact same things?

3. Do you think eternal hell a just punishment for scorning or ignoring God's offer of eternal fellowship with him? Why or why not?

4. Knowing the anger intentionally scorning God's love causes and the heartache growing sin causes, what do you think we should do in our personal lives?

Chapter 4:

The Judge who weeps

"No one can preach the judgments of God accurately without tears in their eyes" – Rev. Paul Anderson, director of harvest communities.

"I had to repent last night," said Caring Christian.

"What happened?" asked Wise Willie.

"I intended to read the book of Lamentations for the first time as an expression of my anger towards God. Yet as I read through it, I found a shocking surprise. Even as I read about God weeping over the pain Israel was suffering, I felt God weeping over what I was suffering."

Caring Christian crooned, "So how can someone experience good life circumstances and still be under the wrath of God? Meanwhile, I'm in terrible circumstances, and yet the Bible and the Holy Spirit tell me that God still cares for me. I am now more confused than ever."

"Do you remember the trip to India a few months ago?" asked, Wise Willie. "Before going on that mission trip, you had to get a hepatitis shot."

"I remember that," said Caring Christian, wincing in pain. "Ouch, did that ever hurt for a moment. Yet that mission trip to India was a once-in-a-lifetime awesome experience. Over that month, I remember seeing God's power in extraordinary ways- even through my weak faith. That God would use me in healing that poor lady's back is still unthinkable to me."

"Did you also remember what happened to Presumptuous Pete?" asked, Wise Willie.

"Yeah, I remember now", said Caring Christian. "Poor Presumptuous Pete; he didn't think he needed the Hepatitis shot. He bragged to us about it. Sure enough, he caught a bad case of Hepatitis a week into the India trip and had to go home. He missed the best part of the trip and still struggles with long-term health effects of the disease."

Wise Willie continued, "Before you got into this mess, I told you that God cares for you from an eternal perspective. What if from an eternal perspective, God was like that medical doctor, giving you a shot?"

The whirlwind of God's emotions

So far, we are encountering a whirlwind of the emotions of God behind his judgments. First, God delights in exalting righteousness in the midst of the fellowship of the Father, Son, and Holy Spirit. All of God's judgments in the courts of heaven and on earth are not about vengeance but the joy of exalting and establishing righteousness. God burns with desire for you and me to join the fellowship of righteousness, peace, and joy found in communion with God.

However, humanity has collectively said "no" as the result of sin, scorning the goodness of God. Sin is more than a little bit of dirt on my "robes of righteousness", it is a malignant cancer ending in eternal destruction and unending agony. God's pure anger is revealed against sin and the terrible impact it has against the people he loves.

God's wrath is fully unleashed against unrepentant sin. He simply withdraws his influence upon people and allows the law of sin and death to run its course on individuals and groups of all sizes (up to nations) without intervening. God's justice is revealed in that he gives everyone what they both want and deserve. In practicing wickedness, people are unknowingly inviting God to repay them with eternal retribution.

God doesn't need anything from us-God is completely satisfied in fellowship of Father, Son, and Holy Spirit. Yet underneath the anger of God towards wickedness and sin burns God's holy jealousy, a burning desire for people to return and have fellowship with him. With long-suffering, God silently waits for people to return to him. Anger is not the only emotion that God expresses in judgment against sin and wickedness.

After Adam and Eve ate from the tree of knowledge of good and evil their eyes were suddenly opened. Once clothed with the majesty and glory of God, they were now self-conscious and afraid. The serpent who had tempted Adam and Eve was now surely taunting them as the icy sting of sin began to physically affect the Garden of Eden.

Paradise was no longer a perfect paradise. Things that were once completely beautiful and alive were now under the law of sin and death. God had warned that if they ate from the tree of the knowledge of good and evil, they would surely die. As the result, they hid from God, covering themselves with fig leaves to shield their nakedness.

The God who wept in Genesis 3:

Out of fear and shame due to their self-centered act, Adam and Eve hid from God. We can find God's reaction to man's sin in Genesis 3:

But the LORD God called to the man, "Where are you?" (Genesis 3:9)

Of course God knows everything- all the treasures of wisdom and knowledge are found in Christ Jesus. When God asks questions, he is not asking for information.

God's questions had a different purpose. The real issue: did Adam know where he was (and how deeply he had already fallen)? It was the beginning of God's operation to bring restoration.

Knowing what had happened in the garden, Adam and Eve were now standing in front of God. There was no where to run, no where to hide. Perhaps with tears streaming down his face, God asked:

"Who told you that you were naked? Have you eaten from the tree that I commanded you not to eat from?" (Genesis 3:11)

The bitter sorrow in God's heart was something Adam and Eve had never experienced. Adam had never known anything except the pleasures of unbroken communion with God. Now after eating from that tree, Adam was confronted with the overwhelming hurt and injustice he had caused in the heart of God. Fellowship with God was broken. Surely justice meant that painful and devastating retribution was coming.

When Adam was confronted with God's sorrow and displeasure about eating from the tree of the knowledge of good and evil, Adam followed up with another self-centered act. Defensive, he did what almost every other man has done throughout history. He bitterly blamed someone else for the trouble. In this case Adam blamed both God and the woman. Under the heat of God's displeasure, Eve did

77

the same thing. She accused and blamed the snake for deceiving her.

The serpent was also forced to attend that meeting. Fully expecting something terrible for eating from the forbidden tree, God began explaining the consequences to Adam and Eve: 1.) There would be spiritual warfare between the seed/offspring of the woman and the "seed" of satan. 2.) There would be disruption and pain in bearing children and human relationships. 3.) Humanity would face a physical environment (both visible and invisible) that is hostile due to the impacts of sin. 4.) As a last line of mercy, God warned of direct intervention through devastating supernatural judgment. God has used these intervention strategies throughout human history to turn humanity from wickedness.

All of these terrible interventions from God would contribute to cause Adam to eventually return to the dust-physical death. Surprisingly, God demonstrated that he was still for Adam and Eve, after what they had done to break his heart. God did not give them over to their sin. God did not outright reject them. He did not instantly kill them for their sin and consign them to an eternity of agony. Scripture says:

The LORD God made garments of skin for Adam and his wife and clothed them. (Genesis 3:21)

The "garments of skin" came from some poor animal-possibly a lamb as God took a sword and killed it. Before a horrified Adam and Eve, perhaps the lamb gave an agonizing screech in pain before breathing his last as a demonstration of the terrible consequences of sin. In that horrible moment, our Great High Priest was also giving a prophetic demonstration that he would one day directly intervene to cover the terrible consequences of sin.

On that devastating day, one last hope remained: Adam and Eve had not eaten from the tree of life. God had warned that if they ate from the tree of the knowledge of good and evil, they would die. If they were now to eat from the tree of life, they would live forever in their broken, sin-infested condition without a solution. The growth and maturing of sin would bring them down into utter destruction and torment that they would live in forever.

This was a crisis of universal proportions requiring drastic intervention. In the counsel of the LORD, with "the serpent" present, God made the sad decree:

And the LORD God said, "The man has now become like one of us, knowing good and evil. He must not be allowed to reach out his hand and take also from the tree of life and eat, and live forever." So the LORD banished him from the Garden of Eden to work the ground from which he had been taken. After he drove the man out, he placed on the east side of the Garden of Eden cherubim and a flaming sword flashing back and forth to guard the way to the tree of life. (Genesis 3:22-24)

Broken-hearted, Adam and Eve were forced to leave the Garden of Eden never to return for their own good. What had been easy and painless was now burdensome and painful. The functions of life that were effortless would now be met with oppressive resistance.

Why did God bring down such a long-term, devastating judgment? Was it out of vengeance and retribution? In the last chapter, we observed what would have happened if God had done nothing. Like malignant cancer, wickedness would have grown into fullness bringing endless destruction. The lake of fire is the final expression of the fullness of sin and its just retribution.

In bringing such long-term devastating consequences, God was like the doctor who hates cancer, and orders agonizing chemo therapy and radiation treatments to preserve life until a cure can be found. For cancer patients, such treatments have devastating side effects they live with.

Through the painful consequences, God was putting roadblock after roadblock to sin-sick humanity falling down slippery slope of depravity that leads to destruction. God would release painful interventions, and even devastating judgments to slow the overall progress of sin in the human race. God outlined his intervention plan when he pronounced his judgments in the garden. Let's look take a look at the differing types of intervention God promised to use from Genesis 3.

Intervention #1: God declares war against satan for us.

Genesis 3 began with the serpent that deceived Eve. Striking at the origin of the fall, God first turned to the snake with sorrow and anger. In righteous indignation, God made a promise to that ancient serpent in the form of a riddle:

So the LORD God said to the serpent, "Because you have done this, Cursed are you above all the livestock and all the wild animals! You will crawl on your belly and you will eat dust all the days of your life. And I will put enmity between you and the woman, and between your offspring and hers; he will crush your head, and you will strike his heel." (Genesis 3:14-15)

The promise was not that God would eventually defeat satan. God promised that he would go to war and defeat satan *on behalf of fallen humanity.* Indeed the promise was that someone completely human would crush satan. This probably further infuriated satan as redemption was not offered to him and the angels that fell.

Hidden within this passage was also the origination of infirmity and disease. Satan was cursed above all of creation. However, he was told that he would eat dust all of his life. Meanwhile, Adam was later told that he is (physically) only dust. In other words, he would be subjected to "the god of this world" who would consume Adam and his off-spring with further sin, suffering, sickness, disease, and eventually death.

Western society sees sickness as the result of trouble in the natural realm, such as germs and a lack of clean water. However, much sickness and disease is also caused by demons, or by emotional and physical stress caused by demonically inspired plots. Sickness is not simply just a chemical or biological issue.

As discussed in the last chapter, when God pours out his wrath upon an individual, a group, or a nation; God simply gives them over, creating a spiritual vacuum. Into the vacuum, satan and his fallen angels who hate people, enter the void and bring emotional, mental, and physical torment. Unknowingly, satan and the demonic realm in their hatred and zeal to hasten the destruction of humanity, become unwitting agents of God's redemptive judgment strategy. The threat of torment by satan and demons are part of God's mercy strategy as a painful roadblock to stop humanity's downward spiral unto destruction.

Satan will never have the last word as he is still subject to the authority of God. As a temporal judgment of God on individuals and cultures, satan's torment is now reversible because of the blood of Jesus. Through repentance and the cross, people can be set free from satanic oppression.

Before Jesus came, the demonic could invade people without remedy if there was persistent or willful sin. God gave Israel instruction and dire warnings related to what was "accursed" (behavior that invites the torment of demons). Jesus came to set the captives free from torment. Yet people still choose selfishness and darkness, worshipping gods and interacting with demons that can never satisfy their deepest desires.

Understanding the celestial conflict behind the scenes:

God had given authority to Adam and Eve with the command to subdue the entire earth-and everything on it under God. Unknown to Adam and Eve at that time, a celestial adversary had been cast to earth:

You were blameless in your ways from the day you were created till wickedness was found in you. Through your widespread trade, you were filled with violence and you sinned. So I drove you in disgrace from the mount of God and I expelled you, O guardian cherub, from among the fiery stones. Your heart became proud on account of your beauty, and you corrupted your wisdom because of your splendor. So I threw you to the earth; I made a spectacle of you before kings. (Ezekiel 28:15-17)

Under God's authority, Adam and Eve were to rule in the midst of God's enemies and make known the supremacy of God's righteous wisdom in producing peace, joy, and every other pleasure.

Outside the understanding of Adam and Eve, satan arrogantly accused God that his wisdom and ways (selfishness at the expense of others) was superior to God's wisdom (centered around humility and servant-hood). Before angelic kings in God's royal court, satan brazenly challenged God's wisdom. Up to 1/3rd of all the angelic hosts of heaven believed satan and thus rebelled against God. Satan's original sin of self-centered pride and arrogant conceit divided heaven and brought untold sorrow in the heavens and on the earth. One of satan's primary goals is to stir up arrogant pride in the human heart- the antithesis of the heart of God.

Satan cannot compete with God in terms of power. The difference in available power and authority between Creator God and any creature (whether it be an archangel or an ant) is endless. God could easily destroy satan and his hordes- but that would not answer the question before the high courts of heaven and the earth: Is God's wisdom was indeed superior to satan's wisdom? Is there a way to prove God's wisdom is supreme in producing pleasure outside the Triune God?

God made human beings in his image with a dream in his heart for us. His original intent was that we would make known the manifold wisdom of God to all of creation: We are the ones who have the honor from God to prove that his wisdom in humility is supreme over satan's wisdom or arrogant pride *regardless of the circumstances.*

Intervention #2: relational difficulty, and conflict

Next, the LORD turned to the woman who had listened to the serpent and first ate from the tree of the knowledge of good and evil. Unlike the serpent, God did not curse the woman (and permit demons to torment her). Instead, scripture tells us:

To the woman he said, "I will greatly increase your pains in childbearing; with pain you will give birth to children. Your desire will be for your husband, and he will rule over you." (Genesis 3:16)

As a consequence of eating of the tree of the knowledge of good and evil, there would be pain and frustration in existing relationships (with Adam) and pain involved in new human relationships for Adam and Eve.

Due to sin, Eve (and Adam) would live with occasional relational conflict and disharmony. Adam and Eve already had a problem after openly eating of the tree of the knowledge of good and evil. Since the first "family feud" in the Garden of Eden, men and women have been trying to usurp each other to be "the top dog". Even those on Jesus' chosen leadership team were always vying for the top positions of honor.

God introduced the source of much of the relational conflict: God had chosen the woman's husband to rule over her. God loves everyone with all his heart. Yet in many ways, it appears that God picks favorites related to special roles. Due to human conceit and bitter envy, we conclude that God loves some more than others.

Ever since the Garden of Eden, God continues to choose individuals and specific people groups for special roles in redemptive history. Some are given much honor in the eyes of men-and be given authority over other people, access to many resources, and great opportunity. Others are given very little. Due to the disaster in Eden and our resulting fleshly nature, it appears to human eyes that God's justice is warped.

The "chosen"/ "not chosen" dynamics related to influence and authority over people often causes relational trouble. Emotional pain, distress, and the further deterioration of human relationships is part of the consequence of sin. The current conflict in the Middle East that threatens to explode into World War III originated in siblings arguing about who had the "birthright". Who has been chosen by God for a special role of honor in redemptive human history?

Adam and Eve saw the bitter harvest of relational conflict and injustice manifested in their children and grandchildren. The original mandate to rule over the earth and subdue it was now subject to perversion. Instead of self-sacrificing servant ruler-ship leading to righteousness, peace, and joy, Adam and Eve chose self-centered ruler-ship at the expense of others. The result of that choice was leadership in this age usually oppresses others leading to bitterness.

Meanwhile, persistent bitterness and unforgiveness opens doors of opportunity for demonic forces to invade and bring unimaginable destruction personally, in families, communities, cities, and even whole nations. In extreme cases, God permits systematic bloodshed through military conflict and war (often inspired by satan and the kingdom of darkness) as judgment upon the nations.

The consequence of relational brokenness at any level (from personal conflict all the way to war and the mass-shedding of blood) do not have to be the final word. God had designed us to represent God on the earth-to each other in righteousness, honor, and joy. The blame-shifting and bitterness out of human self-centeredness were the exact opposite of what God had intended. Thousands of years later in a different garden, Jesus prayed:

My prayer is not for them alone, I pray also for those who will believe in me through their message, that all of them may be one, Father, just as you are in me and I am in you. May they also be in us so that the world may believe that you have sent me. (John 17:20-21)

Self-centeredness in the Garden of Eden was the original root of relational conflict. The humility of Jesus displayed at the cross is the root of relational healing. Through preferring one another, and honoring each other by the grace of God, the consequence of relational difficulty, pain, and conflict from the garden could be reversed and healed. However only by meeting at the foot of the cross together can the deepest relational conflict be reconciled.

The second consequence Eve faced was extreme pain in child birth. Indeed, in the next chapter the scripture says that Eve gave birth to Abel. Scripture records Eve saying,

"With the help of the LORD I have brought forth a man." (Genesis 4:1)

From other passages of scripture and even human history, we know that childbirth was an extremely difficult and agonizingly painful event for women. One mother named his baby boy "Jabez" because of the pain involved. Many have even died in the process of childbirth throughout history. The pain was so intense that it caused Eve (and many others) to cry out to the LORD for help.

Underneath the consequence of extreme pain of childbirth in Genesis 3 was a hidden great hope. God had promised that the seed of the woman would eventually crush the serpent's head.

After great pain and effort, mothers say there is nothing more satisfying than touching eternity and bringing forth a child who will live for ever in the image of God. Jesus said,

"A woman giving birth to a child has pain because her time has come; but when her baby is born she forgets the anguish because of her joy that a child is born into the world." (John 16:21)

Each heart knows its own bitterness, and no one else can share its joy. (Proverbs 14:10)

Beneath the consequence of extreme pain is the promise of the joy of redemption. The joy of overcoming to bring forth life swallows up the pain of labor. Jabez turned the pain in his life into something noble through seeking

God. In other words, the joy in the end was going to make all the extreme pain and sorrow worth it.

Intervention #3: Creation groans

Finally, God turned to Adam. This is the man God had blessed with authority to fill the earth and subdue it. However, because of his unbelief he unwittingly chose a different authority in eating the forbidden fruit. With disobedience (through eating of the tree of the knowledge of good and evil), came terrible consequences to everything God gave under his authority. Scripture said,

To Adam he said, "Because you listened to your wife and ate from the tree about which I commanded you, 'You must not eat of it,'

"Cursed is the ground because of you; through painful toil you will eat of it all the days of your life. It will produce thorns and thistles for you, and you will eat the plants of the field. By the sweat of your brow you will eat your food until you return to the ground, since from it you were taken; for dust you are and to dust you will return." (Genesis 3:17-19)

Adam disobeyed God's command to eat from the Tree of the Knowledge of Good and Evil. Now creation would do like-wise, resisting Adam (and the rest of humanity) as they exerted their will to subdue creation.

Originally, God desires to share his government and counsel with creation-including mere men on the earth. The Psalmist wrote:

The highest heavens belong to the LORD, but the earth he has given to men. (Psalm 115:16)

In time and space, our Sovereign God and King deliberately shared his government (delegated authority and responsibility) with his creation. With the freedom to participate in God's government (along with responsibility) comes freedom to rebel, with real negative consequences.

Before the fall of Genesis 3, Adam and Eve ruled the earth under the leadership of God in complete purity and innocence. Through obedience to God, Adam's authority reflected the wisdom and righteousness of God to all creation. The Garden of Eden was in peace in a state of wellness and wholeness.

However, in taking the serpent's counsel, Adam and Eve had unwittingly given the authority over the earth to serpent cast down to the earth when they ate from the tree of knowledge of good and evil. Instead of gaining greater authority, they were deceived into live under satan's authority (who has always been under God's authority). No longer was satan and the fallen angels simply a foe to be stomped on in the midst of joyous fellowship and government with God. Instead, satan now had legal authority over the entire earth and the human race to steal, kill, and destroy because Adam gave it to him.

The consequences upon creation were immediate and terrible. Even scientists talk about the law of entropy: left to itself, an orderly system will descend into chaos and disorder. For example, if you have a child (or been a child), you know that a child's room seems to naturally get messy without any effort. The kid needs to clean it up- put focused, skilled energy into setting things back in order. The kid (or you) probably wanted to clean things up by simply setting off a few "explosions" in the room. Such explosions didn't help but just accelerated the descent into mayhem in the room or the whole house.

Before modern science understood the laws of thermodynamics, the Bible gave understanding to the issues. The apostle Paul wrote,

I consider that our present sufferings are not worth comparing with the glory that will be revealed in us. The creation waits in eager expectation for the sons of God to be revealed. For the creation was subjected to frustration, not by its own choice, but by the will of the one who subjected it, in hope that the creation itself will be liberated from its bondage to decay and brought into the glorious freedom of the children of God.

We know that the whole creation has been groaning as in the pains of childbirth right up to the present time. (Romans 8:18-22)

Earth and our immediate environment reflect the groan of creation due to the injustice of sin of the inhabitants of the earth.

For example, under our feet tectonic plates such as the Pacific Rim put tremendous pressure on seismic faults as they grind into each other. The pressure builds and builds until finally, the fault cannot take any more pressure and there is a sudden release in the form of a massive earthquake. Often the result is devastating to cities and even whole regions of the earth as creation groans yet again.

While a massive earthquake eases pressure on one area in the system of tectonic plates, it often causes greater imbalance in other areas of the earth and greatly increases the pressure in another geographical area. Soon enough, one earthquake helps the pressure to build to trigger another one in the earth.

The same thing happens in the weather patterns. Violent storms are the result of imbalances of air pressure, moisture, and temperature. High pressure pushes air away and low pressure takes air in creating the wind. The end result is the painful groans of creation: destructive floods, hurricanes, tornadoes, blizzards, and extreme heat or cold. In futile attempts to return to a peaceful state of equilibrium and balance, creation forms other imbalances that build and provide the foundation for more painful groans.

In his mercy, God has been working and restraining the natural decay of creation. Without God's mercy earth would have spiraled into chaos long-ago. God warned Israel that if they went astray and served other gods, the land would literally vomit them out. God himself warned that he would discipline the people through the created order. Throughout history, we find set times when God released drought and other "natural disasters" to discipline the nation of Israel.

However, this type of extremely painful intervention by God is also sometimes avoidable through repentance. There are many cases in church history and in the Bible where destruction was averted because the people chose to repent. The famous verses quoted to inspire prayer for revival are literal:

When I shut up the heavens so that there is no rain, or command locusts to devour the land or send a plague among my people, if my people who are called by my name will humble themselves and pray and seek my face and turn from their wicked ways, then will I hear from heaven and will forgive their sin and will heal their land. (2 Chronicles 7:13-14)

Even in recent history as documented by George Otis Jr. The land would literally not produce food due to idolatry (and associated witchcraft) and bloodshed in the land. However, when the people repented and turned to the LORD, the land became fertile and fruitful again. From the Canadian Tundra to Fiji to Guatemala, the testimony of creation continues. God responds to his people.

The God who hides his judgments

In most cases, the judgments of God are not easily discerned. There are plenty of other natural, relational, or scientific explanations for events that cause pain and sorrow for humanity. Human dynamics (including military conflicts) are often in play. God can act in human history while remaining veiled. When God walked the earth, most did not recognize him.

Before the age of scientific method and discovery, natural events such as droughts, famines, pestilence, and storms were all viewed as direct judgments of God. However, in modern and post-modern society, such events can be explained using natural, scientific means. Again, in many cases, God's judgments remain hidden.

In another case, the Civil War looks like it was a war to preserve the Union. The south was trying to secede from the north. Issues such as economics, slavery, states rights, and perceived oppression of individual states are often cited as the reasons for the Civil War. The northern states had far more resources and people than the south. The war should have been very short.

Yet, for "some reason", the war raged on costing hundreds of thousands of casualties and untold suffering in the South and the North. Both sides called on God and a revival spirit ripped through both camps. Both sides thought their cause was just. As the Civil War raged on in American history, Abraham Lincoln carefully discerned the judgment of God behind the war related to centuries of slavery, and the associated oppression, and death. He said:

The Almighty has his own purposes. Fondly do we hope--fervently do we pray--that this mighty scourge of war may speedily pass away. Yet, if God wills that it continue, until all the wealth piled up by the bondsman's two-hundred and fifty years of unrequited toil shall be sunk, and until every drop of blood drawn with the lash, shall be repaid by another drawn by the sword, as was said three-thousand years ago, so still it must be said "the judgments of the Lord are true and righteous altogether."

It was on Palm Sunday, 1865 after the customary 40 days of repentance and fasting associated with lent, that the Civil War finally ended.

Intervention #4: Direct acts of supernatural judgment

If Adam would have eaten from the tree of life after eating from the tree of the knowledge of good and evil, all hope of redemption would have been destroyed. In banishing Adam and Eve from the Garden of Eden, God set guardian angels that people could see with flashing swords of fire to prevent them from eating from the tree of life in their fallen state. In an open show of force on that horrible day, God was displaying his last line of mercy: If necessary, God will directly intervene on behalf of humanity in awesome, supernatural judgments to preserve his redemptive plans for the whole of the human race.

God still directly intervenes in awesome miraculous acts of judgment for the whole world to see to protect his redemptive plan for humanity. God warned Noah and then sent the flood to preserve true humanity in the midst of the hellish chaos on the earth. God's tears filled the heavens and the earth for forty days and nights. God destroyed Sodom and Gomorrah in a fiery cataclysm due to the depths of perverse passion in his promised land. God released awesome judgments against the gods of Egypt in the form of plagues to set Israel free to worship him and eventually bring forth the Messiah after 400 years of slavery. The impenetrable walls of Jericho collapsed and the sun stood still to push God's redemptive plan forward. The nations of the earth watched and trembled.

Another thing that makes these miraculous acts of judgment more direct than simply "creation's groan" is that God told his friends, the prophets what he would do and a little bit of why he would do it. God called Abraham a prophet. Regarding the great wickedness of Sodom and the cities of the plain God said:

"Shall I hide from Abraham what I am about to do? Abraham will surely become a great and powerful nation, and all the nations of the earth will be blessed through him. For I have chosen him, so that he will direct his children and his household after him to keep the way of the LORD by doing what is right and just, so that the LORD will bring about for Abraham what he has promised him." (Genesis 18:17-19)

In Sodom, sin had matured and reached such horrible depths that there was no other remedy available. Everything else (including captivity and redemption through Abraham in Genesis 14) did not turn their hearts. The demonized inhabitants were bitterly hell-bent on violent, perverse sin. Their proximity to Abraham and influence were a direct threat to God's global plan to bring redemption. Thus with tears, God gave the cities of the plain the fullness of what they were obstinate in choosing.

When whole nations or societies pervert justice and righteousness, God sent messengers to warn the people to turn back to righteousness. If they did not repent, God then intervened with small disasters while continuing to warn them through his messengers. Finally, God eventually intervened with devastating effects for the sake of human redemption. God judged whole nations by giving them over to the consequences of idolatry and bloodshed. They drank the cup of his wrath leading to delusional arrogance and complacency. Meanwhile simultaneously, God silently raised up others to conquer the deluded society as agents of judgment.

Sadly, even unprepared upright people get hurt (or killed) in the midst of God's corporate judgments. Lot barely escaped with his life, but lost everything. Jesus is the man of sorrows who weeps over our suffering caused by his painful interventions.

In the New Testament, Acts 11-13 describes the drama that unfolded related to beginning God's world-wide gospel mission to the nations through Peter, Paul, and Barnabas. A drought predicted by the prophet Agabus caused Barnabas and Paul to go to Jerusalem to bring supplies. Herod killed James, and attempted to kill Peter. Satan then moved his pawn Herod north from Judea to Caesarea to stop Paul and Barnabas from launching their mission. Puffed up and irrevocably arrogant, God struck down Herod as he was eaten with worms and God's world-wide mission movement went forth from Antioch. As the result, people from many nations now rejoice at the proclamation of the Gospel of the Kingdom.

Jesus warned that in the days immediately before his return, sin will reach perverse depths not seen since the days of Noah. Genesis 6 describes the days of Noah-where in many cases, life on earth was beginning to imitate life in hell. Isaiah wrote of those terrible days:

My soul yearns for you in the night; in the morning my spirit longs for you. When your judgments come upon the earth, the people of the world learn righteousness. Though grace is shown to the wicked, they do not learn righteousness; even in a land of uprightness they go on doing evil and regard not the majesty of the LORD. O LORD, your hand is lifted high, but they do not see it. Let them see your zeal for your people and be put to shame; let fire reserved for your enemies consume them. (Isaiah 26:9-11)

In response to the fullness of wickedness on the earth and for the sake of his beloved ones, the awesome and terrible judgments described in the book of Revelation will be released. These terrible acts of judgment will be God's final severe mercy to turn people from perdition before it is too late.

The Judge who weeps:

As the judge of all the earth, God delights in exalting the wisdom of righteousness over wickedness. With burning desire, God desires people to enter into the joy and peace of fellowship with him in purity, humility, and righteousness. Beginning with Adam and Eve, humanity gave a collective "no" to God. Aligned with satan, we preferred to exalt ourselves above fellowship with God-spurning his love, provoking him to anger. Heartbroken and angry, God's could have given humanity as a whole over to the progressive, malignant power of sin that grows unto eternal torment and destruction. Yet immediately, God began pursuing humanity to stop their destructive path to perdition.

From the beginning, God never intended people to experience weeping, suffering, and pain. In the midst of the destruction of Jerusalem and Babylonian captivity, Jeremiah wrote in faith:

For men are not cast off by the Lord forever. Though he brings grief, he will show compassion, so great is his unfailing love. For he does not willingly bring affliction or grief to the children of men. (Lamentation 3:31-33)

Contrary to how much of popular culture portrays God, the Bible says God was heart broken over the humiliation and the suffering of his people going into Babylonian captivity. God expressed his feelings through Jeremiah:

Oh, that my head were a spring of water and my eyes a fountain of tears! I would weep day and night for the slain of my people. (Jeremiah 9:1)

In every case, God did not delight in bringing judgment when it meant his image-bearers would suffer and die. With tears, God allowed people who had rebelled to die and receive what they had chosen for themselves for all eternity. With more tears, God allowed some of those who had chosen him to suffer and die at the hands of evil men as an expression of his devastating corporate judgment upon the whole nation.

Even after the Babylonian captivity, God had been warning the Jewish people that trouble was coming in the form of another captivity at the hands of 'the people of the prince to come' through the prophet Daniel. Before the destruction, yet again God offered the merciful alternative related to Mark 16:15-20, Matthew 28:18-20, and Acts 1:8. If the city of Jerusalem had believed Jesus, obeyed his commission, and gone out preaching the good news to every nation, there would not have been much to destroy in Jerusalem in AD 70. History could have been vastly different. Yet the people generally did not listen to Jesus, and receive him as their Messiah:

As he approached Jerusalem and saw the city, he wept over it and said, "If you, even you, had known on this day what would bring you peace-but now it is hidden from your eyes. (Luke 19:41-42)

God had offered mercy and peace through submitting to his righteousness. However most of the inhabitants of the city refused his path unto peace and joy, breaking the heart Jesus because he knew what would come next.

After Jesus' resurrection in the New Testament, Paul was zealous for the kingdom of God to come to Israel, but completely misguided. After Paul encountered Jesus the righteous judge on the road to Damascus, he later wrote:

*I speak the truth in Christ-I am not lying, my
conscience confirms it in the Holy Spirit- I have great
sorrow and unceasing anguish in my heart. For I could
wish that I myself were cursed and cut off from Christ
for the sake of my brothers, those of my own race, the
people of Israel. (Romans 9:1-4)*

The apostle Paul carried the heart of Jesus for the Jewish
people. The heartache Jesus shared with Paul was so
great that like Moses, the apostle Paul tried to cut a deal:
He would go to hell for eternity if the people would be
redeemed. How much more the anguish and the pain in
the heart of Jesus for those who would die in the judgment
and be ushered into the fullness of what they had "wanted"
through their vile actions? Again, Jesus wept.

Discussion questions:

1. If God had done nothing, but let Adam and Eve live in sin, what do you think would have happened?

2. How do difficulty, sorrow, and pain restrain the growth and spread of sin?

3. From chapter 2, we recall that God delights in exalting righteousness. How can the God who delights in exalting righteousness also weep in sorrow at his judgments?

4. From chapter 3, How does God's sorrow and anguish differ from God's anger?

5. As someone who loves Jesus the Judge, how do you think we can bring comfort to his heart if you understand this about him?

Chapter 5

Do Justly: The Judge who delegates

"The only thing necessary for the triumph of evil is for good men to do nothing"- Edmund Burke.

"I'm so frustrated with Swindler Sam, so I did something about it. I went to the city police to file a complaint," said Caring Christian. "I was hoping the city would do something to get my money back, but the city government said that they couldn't do anything."

"So now I'm even more angry and confused" continued Caring Christian. "God is the ultimate judge, yet God delegates much of the administration of his justice to people."

"Yes", said Wise Willie. "God entrusts people to administrate justice."

"What about when people get it wrong and deliberately practice injustice like it seems Swindler Sam and the city government is doing? The poor victims of injustice will never see justice done. Meanwhile, people like Swindler Sam get away with it."

"There is always a day of reckoning for the city and for Swindler Sam", said Wise Willie. "The real challenge is whether you can trust in God's ultimate justice and continue to seek righteousness and justice. There is a day of reckoning coming for you as well."

"The whole mess with Swindler Sam has made me question God's justice. I don't think even you can answer for God," added Caring Christian.

"I'm not even going to try," replied Wise Willie. "However, you are faced with a choice. Are you going to continue to seek justice and righteousness, fight the bitterness, and trust Jesus as your judge or are you going to seek justice your own way."

Fellowship through delegated authority

Ever since the beginning, God has intended people in his image to share the government with him. God blessed Adam with the original mandate to rule from Genesis 1:26-28. With this governmental freedom comes responsibility to actually participate in the government. True loyalty must be chosen. Adam had been given governmental responsibility for the earth- but the task was too much for even him. God deliberately designed the nature of dominion over creation as a means to greater fellowship and intimacy with him.

Even from the beginning, God's instructions and commandments were meant to expose our need for him and draw us into fellowship. God gave Adam the commandment to rule over the earth:

"Be fruitful and increase in number; fill the earth and subdue it. Rule over the fish of the sea and the birds of the air and over every living creature that moves on the ground." (Genesis 1:28)

From the beginning, God wanted humanity to enjoy ruling the earth in fellowship with him. God wanted man to enjoy righteousness and justice with him.

While the government of God has always been a theocracy, God delegates authority to his "chosen" of creation. God gives the government of the earth to people- including power to delegate when he placed Adam in the garden. With governmental authority comes responsibility (with consequences). If we are put "in charge" with freedom to choose along with certain accountability for our actions, the first thing we need is an action plan to administrate our governing responsibilities.

Meanwhile, Adam began with absolutely no knowledge, but with the abilities to acquire wisdom and knowledge quickly. Wouldn't it make sense to seek out help from "someone" who is always present, overwhelmingly kind, has all the knowledge and authority to do anything, is incredibly wise, knows what is best for us, and is zealous that it would go well for us? Who wouldn't desire to fully agree with a government like this- now or in all of eternity? Who wouldn't want to know this "someone" in a genuinely personal way? Spiritual and physical government was another way to bring forth fellowship with God, righteousness, joy, and pleasure.

From the beginning, our humble God desired fellowship and joy for us. However, God did not want robots. What God wanted from humanity had to be freely chosen by humanity-implying the option and risk that people would choose no. In setting the tree of knowledge of good and evil in the garden, God set up a daily test and opportunity to prove Adam's loyalty to God:

And the LORD commanded the man, "You are free to eat from any tree in the garden; but you must not eat from the tree of the knowledge of good and evil, for when you eat of it you will surely die." (Genesis 2:16-17)

Would Adam seek understanding and knowledge apart from God or would he wait for the times when God walked in the cool of the evening? Every day, he was faced with a daily choice to depend on God for understanding (that would only come on God's timing in communion) or eat from the tree of the knowledge of good and evil. When Adam ate from the tree of the knowledge of good and evil, he committed high treason before the court of heaven- joining with satan's rebellion.

Do justly: God's instructions to maximize fellowship.

Even after the fall, God still wanted fellowship with broken, fallen humanity. Even though others were unjust and unfaithful, God remained faithful to his original intentions. God did not take governmental stewardship and leadership over the earth from people. While God reserved the right to intervene as the sovereign over the universe, God still included us in on his justice system. Both individually over our own lives and corporately, God left people in charge over the lives of others and the rest of creation. Indeed, in setting up roadblocks to prevent the increase of sin, God involved us in administrating order and doing justice.

However, God gives moral instructions to show how we can walk in a measure of wisdom, joy, and peace in this age. They direct us towards enjoying a measure of fellowship with God today as we look forward to God's restoration to bring wholeness. His instructions show how we can cooperate with God's process of restoration. The psalmist wrote:

The law of the LORD is perfect, reviving the soul. The statutes of the LORD are trustworthy, making wise the simple. The precepts of the LORD are right, giving joy to the heart. The commands of the LORD are radiant, giving light to the eyes. (Psalm 19:7-8)

God's counsel through his Word and the Holy Spirit give us understanding on how we can honor and guard this sacred fellowship with God. Through even post-Eden limited fellowship with God, we can firmly resist the malignant nature of sin and its destructive effects.

After the terrifying ordeal when God spoke the 10 commandments openly in an audible voice, the people sent Moses up to the mountain to get more instructions from God. There was need to understand God's heart for justice and righteousness behind his decrees.

God gave moral instructions to us in the Old and New Testament for our own good. Before Jesus came to repair the breach, God told Moses:

See, I have taught you decrees and always as the LORD my God commanded me, so that you may follow them in the land you are entering to take possession of it. Observe them carefully, for this will show your wisdom and understanding to the nations, who will hear about all these decrees and say, "Surely this great nation is a wise and understanding people." What other nation is so great to have their gods near them the way the LORD our God is near us whenever we pray for him? And what other nation is so great as to have such righteous decrees and laws as this body of laws I am setting before you today?
(Deuteronomy 4:5-8)

The debacle in Eden did not change God's ultimate plan. Through following God's instructions, we were all invited into showing fellow humanity along with the angelic realm (currently, not normally visible to people) the superiority of God's humble wisdom to satan's selfish, arrogant wisdom.

Even after the fall, God continued to give us instructions and counsel through his word and the Holy Spirit. He spoke through the prophet Micah:

He has showed you, O man, what is good. And what does the LORD require of you? To act justly and to love mercy and to walk humbly with your God. (Micah 6:8)

The entire Bible is a gold mine of counsel from God for life to work on the earth in this age.

Following the instructions God gave to Moses in the book of Exodus were never meant to earn us salvation- sin had already broken perfect fellowship. Even before the fall into sin, Adam did not and earn acceptance from God by his good works. In the same way, we cannot earn God's acceptance by our good works or rescue ourselves from the consequences of our sin. We are completely at the mercy of God's jealous desire for us. The instructions continue to alert us to the need for God's salvation.

While human obedience could not earn salvation, it was proof before heaven that the Jewish people believed that God would one day intervene to save them from sin. Faith without works was dead. Men and women of God died in faith that God's salvation would one day break in.

In the same way, our obedience to Jesus is proof that our love for God is real, having received what Jesus did to save us from the penalty and the power of sin. Faith without works is dead. God wants to make his wisdom known to the nations of the earth through a people who would carefully follow the Lamb wherever he goes.

Our resources: A personal test

Justice and righteousness have been the foundation of God's leadership or governing authority. Jesus instructed us to seek first the kingdom of God and his righteousness (Matthew 6:33). However, the broader context of this command was a message related to fear, stewardship, and a discussion on money.

In our western culture, we have bought into a lie: We believe that we are our own masters. In the United States, there is such an emphasis on rights: my right to happiness, my right to comfort, my right to do whatever I want. Our culture emphasizes our rights and freedoms that we are supposed to enjoy without responsibility. This mindset of "it's all about me" completely contradicts what the Bible says: Jesus is LORD which means we are not. This immediately brings up two problems:

First, our culture has lost touch with reality. We think that we are the masters of our planet and the environment. Meanwhile, scripture tells us that God (not the devil) owns the earth and everything in it (Psalm 24:1). God is the owner and we are stewards-and meant to be servants. He is either "Lord" or we are operating in rebellion.

Second, we haven't really understood what "Lordship" really means. In medieval times, peasants submitted themselves to a lord for the sake of security, protection from enemies, and help in putting food on the table. However, in submitting themselves to a lord, they were also giving up all of their land rights, their resources, their time, talents, and even their relationships. Everything now belonged to the lord to be used for the lord's purposes. "No, lord" was an oxy-moronic statement.

In saying that "Jesus is LORD", it means that we have freely given up all of our land rights, all of our resources, time, talents, and even relationships to serve Jesus' purposes. The clearest way we (or someone else) can tell that Jesus is truly Lord of our lives is if we 1.) Faithfully follow his general instructions in practicing justice and righteousness 2.) As bond servants, we wisely use the resources, time, talents, relationships, influence, and anything else he gives for the sake of his kingdom.

The common test that God gives everyone in society is related to money and resources. We all need things such as food, water, clothes, and shelter. We all have desires as well. Virtually every society uses some form of money as a medium to exchange goods and services. How are we going to gain wealth and resources? How are we going to spend or use the resources we have? There are over 2,000 verses in scripture than either directly or indirectly address the issue of money and stewardship. The tithe is only 10% of the issue of our overall stewardship of resources before God.

Would we do justly? Practicing lawlessness brings destruction. Practicing justice and righteousness with wisdom leads to greater blessing and responsibility. God delights in exalting righteousness- even in front of our fellow peers to influence them.

Human government mission: Guard the sanctity of life

After the flood in Genesis 6, God gave Noah a covenant promise that was confirmed with the sign of the rainbow: Never again would God send a flood and destroy every living creature. However, God also said:

"But you must not eat meat that has its lifeblood still in it. And for your lifeblood I will surely demand an accounting. I will demand an accounting from every animal. And from each man, too, I will demand an accounting for the life of his fellow man. Whoever sheds the blood of man, by man shall his blood be shed; for in the image of God has God made man. As for you, be fruitful and increase in number; multiply on the earth and increase upon it."(Genesis 9:4-7)

Hidden within the covenant promise was a warning and a challenge. In giving a covenant promise to not wipe all of humanity out, it also implied that people groups would grow and societal structures would be set in place.

God set the cornerstone that human government would be forced to reckon with: the value of human life. Justice must be done to man if he sheds the blood of another man. God was also charging Noah and governmental leaders with upholding justice to prevent the shedding of blood.

In Chapter 3, we looked at how before the flood, God allowed people to live for hundreds of years. Sin ran rampant, relatively un-checked by God's judgments as God allowed the sin of man to almost fully mature before releasing the flood of judgment that covered the earth. In giving the promise that God would not wipe out every living thing on earth again, God warned that he would intervene in overwhelming judgment more quickly upon societies of people to prevent sin from fully maturing in corporate humanity. God confused the languages at Babel dividing people into ethnic groups before humanity could unify in defiance leading to utter destruction.

After delivering his people from Egypt, one of the first things God did was to build governmental leadership in the new nation of Israel (Exodus 18:17-26). Later, Moses wrote:

So I took the leading men of your tribes, wise and respected men and appointed them to have authority over you-as commanders of thousands, of hundreds, of fifties and of tens and as tribal officials. And I charged your judges at the time: Hear the disputes between your brothers and judge fairly, whether the case is between brother Israelites or between one of them and an alien. Do not show partiality in judging; hear both small and great alike. Do not be afraid of any man, for judgment belongs to God. Bring me any case too hard for you, and I will hear it. And at that time I told you everything you were to do.
(Deuteronomy 1:15-18)

God was entrusting part of his justice system on the earth into the hands of men. As men in the image of God, they were to release the judgments upon individuals on behalf of God according to what is written in the instructions.

Later, in instituting the priestly ministry, God specifically linked the priesthood with the government in Deuteronomy 17:8-13. Even as the heavens and the earth are coming together under the leadership of Jesus in perfection when he returns, God always intended the heavenly justice system (through worship and prayer) to come together with the governmental leadership on earth to practice justice. We are specifically instructed to pray for those in authority (1Timothy 2:1-2).

Governmental responsibility: uphold justice

Righteousness and justice are the foundation of God's government. Even in the United States, people take the oath of office to discharge the laws of the land. God specifically raises up leaders for the sake of justice and keeping order:

Everyone must submit himself to the governing authorities, for there is no authority except that which God has established. The authorities that exist have been established by God. Consequently, he who rebels against the authority is rebelling against what God has instituted, and those who do so will bring judgment on themselves. For rulers hold no terror for those who do right, but for those who do wrong. Do you want to be free from fear of the one in authority? Then do what is right and he will commend you. For he is God's servant to do you good. But if you do wrong, be afraid, for he does not bear the sword for nothing. He is God's servant, an agent of wrath to bring judgment on the wrong-doer. (Romans 13:1-4)

The opposite of order is not freedom but lawlessness. Without governmental leadership in society (or in the Church) that upholds righteousness and justice, the result is anarchy, chaos, and lawlessness leading to destruction.

In the earth, many people want positions of leadership or authority for the sake of ruling over others or for the benefits society give people in positions of authority. Even in society, people study for years to become qualified in the eyes of the world to serve in positions of leadership and authority. We are to show ourselves approved.

Indeed, God's word tells us that those in government (especially in the Church, but also in society) who rule well are worthy of "double honor" (1 Timothy 5:16-20). Dealing with many complex issues and human pressure to do what is right and just in God's eyes brings great joy to the kingdom of heaven.

However, in the same way, God warns that those who are put in positions of leadership and authority are more accountable to God than others:

Not many of you should presume to be teachers, my brothers, because you know that we who teach will be judged more strictly. (James 3:1)

Jesus warned of great judgment for those who misused authority and perverted justice:

But if anyone causes one of these little ones in me to sin, it would be better for him to have a large millstone hung around his neck and to be drowned in the depths of the sea. Woe to the world because of the things that cause men to sin! Such things must come, but woe to the man through whom they come! (Matthew 18:6-7)

Those who deliberately lead others into sin are in big trouble before God.

Later, Jesus warned his future apostolic leadership team about heightened judgment for those in authority (especially if backed up by the power of the Holy Spirit):

"Who then is the faithful and wise servant, whom the master has put in charge of the servants in his household to give them their food at the proper time? It will be good for that servant whose master finds him doing so when he returns. I tell you the truth, he will put him in charge of all his possessions. But suppose that servant is wicked and says to himself, 'My master is staying away a long time' and then begins to beat his fellow servants and to eat and drink with drunkards. The master of that servant will come on a day when he does not expect him and at an hour he is not aware of. He will cut him to pieces and assign him a place with the hypocrites, where there will be weeping and gnashing of teeth." (Matthew 24:48-51)

These passages and many others talk about the awesome responsibility to use authority to exalt righteousness and execute justice with God's help.

Yet who is truly up to the task? Ever since the garden, government was never intended to be exercised without dependence upon God. After losing election after election, Abraham Lincoln recognized his need for divine help to do justly. Though he felt he was one of the weakest U.S. Presidents, even secular historians recognize him as one of the greatest.

Poverty and human responsibility before God

Bringing justice to the poor is a key challenge that individuals, government, and the church must face. In terms of talents and ability, God deliberately chooses to give some people more intellectual capacity, strength, and emotional intelligence than other people. As the result, some people end up becoming influential, wealthy, and honored in this age. Others are not wealthy in talent or opportunity in this age. In correcting his disciples' complaints related to Mary of Bethany's extravagant actions, Jesus says that there would always be some who are poor.

An Italian economist Vilfredo Pareto, made the observation of "the vital few" with roughly an 80-20 observation. Regardless of the governmental or economic system a nation used, Pareto observed that roughly 80% of the resources were in the hands of 20% of the people. In business roughly 20% of the customers made up 80% of the business. Again, the result is that some end up vastly richer than others.

In every society on earth, some people will be poor. Poverty is relative. Someone in the United States is considered poor if they make less than $15,000 per year. Someone making $15,000 a year is considered extremely wealthy in the nation of Haiti. On a global scale, anyone living in the United States who is not on the streets should consider themselves wealthy. Someone making only $5,000 a year is in the top 90% in terms of global wealth by some reports.

Relative poverty does not absolve anyone of moral or even financial responsibility. The government and the court system were to judge rich and poor with impartiality- poverty was not a legitimate excuse to sin.

If someone filed a lawsuit against someone else, the courts were to judge the facts of the lawsuit and bring judgment according to the careful findings:

Do not pervert justice; do not show partiality to the poor or favoritism to the great, but judge your neighbor fairly. (Leviticus 19:15)

Whether someone was rich or poor should have no bearing on the outcome of the lawsuit (or criminal charges) before a court of law. Doing justice in a legal sense means that there is no partiality shown. Yet across the earth, systematic injustice is practiced- often based on the color of your skin.

At the root of ethnocentric thinking is a corporate sense of arrogance and entitlement: *Our ethnic group is better than the other ethnic group.* James 3 warned that strife and quarreling begins because of self-centered wisdom. How much more when whole ethnic groups are sucked into believing that they are superior to another? One ethnic group with greater resources and power usually ended up oppressing another one unto bitterness and rage.

God understands the potential destruction of racism. Jesus warned in the last days that many wars would be sparked because one ethnic group would rise up against a different one. At the root of the conflicts are differing value systems and accusations of injustice. In giving the law, justice was to be applied with equity between native-born and foreigner without partiality.

In the agricultural society of the Old Testament, farmers were instructed to only go through their fields only once. They were to leave the gleanings for the poor and the alien. Yet the poor had to actually go out and get the food for themselves. The courts were not to favor the poor in lawsuits simply because they were poor (and the other guy was rich)-but to maintain justice and order equally for everyone.

In the New Testament, Timothy was challenged with the issue of taking care of the widows and orphans. The Church was only to take care of widows and orphans who were clearly in need who did not have family. Families were supposed to take care of their own to promote love and strengthen relationships. Those who were able-bodied were supposed to work and not be idle (2 Thessalonians 3). We were designed to be fruitful, multiply, and take dominion over the earth.

The underlying issue of Paul's instructions to Timothy related to widows and to the Thessalonians was to avoid promoting an entitlement mentality- a derivative of self-centered conceit and a form of destructive pride that leads to bitterness and great trouble. An entitlement mentality says, "because I did __(insert your favorite reason here)__, I deserve _____". In reality, we have been given the greatest gift of all through Christ Jesus: our destiny was changed from eternal condemnation and destruction to eternal life. God lists arrogant haughtiness as one of the things that he hates.

Social safety nets by the church or the government were meant to value and protect human life. When the government promotes entitlement programs simply because some people have less than other people, the result is that people get trapped into the slavery of an entitlement mindset- a form of conceit. Programs that were meant to preserve life end up promoting death through encouraging entitlement and conceit to grow in the hearts of recipients. They were never meant to absolve people of personal responsibility simply because they were "poor" or disadvantaged.

God's test for governments: the helpless in society

However, this brings up a very important question: *What about those who are unable to physically work because of severe disability (developmentally or through injury)?* In many cases, these people are not working not because of lack of desire, but because of lack of ability (mentally or physically). How does the government and especially God's people (the Church) treat those who cannot possibly repay them on a long-term basis?

God used Sodom and the cities of the plain as a solemn warning to other governments that would come after them. The prophet Ezekiel wrote:

Now this was the sin of your sister Sodom: She and her daughters were arrogant, overfed, and unconcerned; they did not help the poor and needy. They were haughty and did detestable things before me. Therefore I did away with them as you have seen. (Ezekiel 16:49-50)

In the rebuke to the nation of Israel, Ezekiel was talking about the same issues among the governmental leadership. The nation had departed from God and was not upholding the sanctity of life even among the poorest of the poor who were helpless.

Hitler used (or misused) the instructions of 2 Thessalonians 3 to justify the involuntary euthanasia to thousands of "worthless eaters" in Germany. The purge spread to other "undesirables" in Germany including homosexuals, Sikh's, Gypsies, and other groups. The population "cleansing" spread to the Jewish people and began to affect millions of others across Europe. By the time everything was done in 1945 when Hitler committed suicide and Germany surrendered, over 50 million people were dead from World War II and the accompanying Holocaust.

Radical evil is not merely a left or right wing governmental issue. Under Joseph Stalin, the USSR killed millions of its own people in the midst of the communist revolution through famine, disease, and repression. Mao's "Cultural Revolution" in China killed millions of Chinese peasants who opposed his rule. Recently, up to 1 million people were killed in Rwanda by the government in retaliation for killing a leader. In every case, it began with a purge of the poor or undesirables in society.

From a humanistic worldview, Hitler and other genocidal governments could justify their actions. In humanism, there is no ultimate Judge. People are the final authority. Among peers, people are only as valuable as what they can contribute to society to make us (or me) better. Hitler was simply "getting rid of" the weak and unwanted in society. Underlying the humanistic justification is the presumption that there is not a God who is a judge and evaluates us. Indeed the issue of human rights cannot be divorced from faith and belief that we are accountable to an ultimate Judge.

While Hitler is dead and gone, the philosophy of humanism continues to plague society. Humanism underpins the practice of abortion of "unwanted babies". Humanistic reasoning calls some pregnancies "unwanted" and gives us the right to abort the problem because of the economic, emotional, and physical trouble it produces.

Of course, this is in sharp contrast to what God says about human life. David wrote in Psalm 139:

For you created my inmost being; you knit me together in my mother's womb. I praise you because I am fearfully and wonderfully made; your works are wonderful, I know that full well. My frame was not hidden from you when I was made in the secret place. (Psalm 139:13-15)

From the life of David, we observe that God can lead people perfectly using unjust human leaders (like King Saul). How much more can God form and fashion life and blessing conceived out of difficult or even completely unjust circumstances?

The same humanistic philosophies drive sexual immorality, the root issue behind human trafficking and the selling of vulnerable women, and children into sexual slavery. Over 30 million people world-wide are bought and sold annually in an underground black market for the sake of sexual gratification. Often the people are allured into bondage because of grinding poverty that threatens their very existence. Organizations such as *Exodus Cry* have done extensive documentaries depicting the horrors these victims face physically, emotionally, and physiologically. In many cases the practice of human trafficking ends in death through abortions, disease, suicide, and plain murder. Yet in the name of religion or humanism these practices are justified for the sake of self-gratification and economic gain.

However as we have seen from God's point of view revealed in scripture, each individual has a value that is beyond what can be measured this side of eternity. Jesus specifically warned against causing any of the little ones to sin (Matthew 18:6). God expects the governments of nations to maintain the value of human life as the cornerstone of their human justice system. God specifically described the practice of human trafficking as one of the reasons he will bring the nations into judgment (Joel 3:3; Revelation 18:13).

The economic value of what people can produce or the biblical sanctity of life: Which value system do we shape our society by? Every government throughout human history must choose their worldview. The blind, the deaf, the lame, the helpless, and the mentally broken are the collision point of these world-views that drive the values of society. God tells us what we are to do:

Seek justice, encourage the oppressed. Defend the cause of the fatherless, plead the case of the widow. (Isaiah 1:17)

Speak up for those who cannot speak for themselves, for the rights of all who are destitute. Speak up and judge fairly; defend the rights of the poor and needy. (Proverbs 31:8-9)

Before we could do anything for God or other people, God loved us and invited us into his eternal society in heaven as image-bearers of God. In showing the kindness and compassion to those who cannot defend or help themselves, we are re-presenting God to them as well as many others.

God holds the leadership particularly accountable:

Out of his zeal for life, God will hold the governments of the nations accountable on the issues related to shedding of innocent blood, the value of human life, and other forms of perverting justice. Even from the beginning, God warned that perverting justice for the poor and vulnerable would bring a curse- God's discipline through demonic oppression of a nation.

Jesus reserved his most severe rebukes for the religious leaders and the governmental leaders of Israel who were leading Israel astray:

Woe to you Pharisees, because you give God a tenth of your mint, rue and all other kinds of garden herbs, but you neglect justice and the love of God. You should have practiced the latter without leaving the former undone. (Luke 11:42)

This was basically the same rebuke that God sent through prophets to Israel:

The LORD enters into judgment against the elders and leaders of his people: "It is you who have ruined my vineyard; the plunder from the poor is in your houses. What do you mean by crushing my people and grinding the faces of the poor?" (Isaiah 3:14-15)

The people of the land practice extortion and commit robbery; they oppress the poor and needy and mistreat the alien, denying them justice. (Ezekiel 22:29)

Clearly, these passages and others indicate that God decisively holds governmental leaders and those with influence at a much higher intensity of accountability. When justice is not done by those God entrusted with authority to do justice, God takes it personally!

In the New Testament Church, God took the mistreatment of the poor even more seriously, bringing discipline more quickly. The Church in Corinth was made up of rich and poor. For the poor, when the people came together, it was perhaps their only opportunity to get a good meal for the whole week. Meanwhile, the rich would get there first with their food and eat without waiting for the poor. The poor would then get there and there was no food left-while the rich were pressuring them to get on with their program, breaking the unity of God's people. Paul in addressing the situation said:

For anyone who eats and drinks without recognizing the body of the Lord eats and drinks judgment on himself. That is why many among you are weak and sick, and a number of you have fallen asleep. (1 Corinthians 11:29-30)

Jesus, the just judge still stands up for the poor in their midst- and requires the leadership in the Church to do the same.

God so loves righteousness and justice that it is a salvation issue for those he places in authority. In essence, those who rule wisely and seek righteousness and justice well will be greatly blessed and favored. Scripture exalted kings and other leaders who ruled with justice and righteousness for all people. While waiting for Jesus to restore perfect justice, we are to seek the Lord for his judgments.

Meanwhile, those in authority who intentionally pervert justice and oppress others for selfish gain will not be with Jesus for all eternity. Confessions of faith to win votes by politicians are meaningless if not demonstrated in works to uphold justice and righteousness. In the United States, those who hold public office take "the oath of office" publicly. In taking an oath in the name of Jesus, they are asking for God's judgments from above to help them. They are also asking for God's wrath upon their own lives should they deliberately pervert righteousness and justice.

God protecting humanity- The rise and fall of nations;

Justice and righteousness through human government is very serious to God. In the case of whole nations or societies who persistently fail to uphold righteousness and justice, sin gets out of control. God eventually intervenes with devastating effects and the whole society vanishes from the pages of history. Often God raised up another society to make war upon and conquer the evil society as an agent of God's corporate judgment. Sadly, many relatively upright people and children get crushed in the midst of God's corporate judgment. Jesus is the man of sorrows who weeps over the suffering caused by people acting (unknowingly) as agents of God's judgment. As far as their eternal destiny, will not the judge of all the earth do what is right? (Genesis 18:25)

For example scripture tells us that God would not allow Israel to return to the land for more than 400 years. In essence, God gave the Amorites and the other inhabitants of the land more than 400 years to repent of arrogant sins leading to idolatry, sorcery, and the shedding of innocent blood (Genesis 14:16-20). Yet in 400 years, instead of turning to the LORD, they turned away from the LORD leading to a maturing in human wickedness, aided by the demonic realm associated with sorcery and idolatry. More than 400 years later, God released Israel to conquer the land as his agent of judgment against people who would not repent where sin had greatly matured in society.

In the case of all Israel, God sent prophet after prophet to warn the people to turn away from idolatry and back to the LORD, the fountain head of righteousness and justice. The prophets also repeatedly warned the people to practice righteousness and justice with each other (especially the poor). Repeatedly his servants warned of his judgments if they did not turn back to the LORD and practice righteousness. If they would not do righteousness and justice that God had entrusted to them, God would directly intervene in (devastating) judgment.

Sadly, Israel generally did not listen. The northern tribes of Israel were carried off into captivity in 722BC. Scripture says why:

They forsook all the commands of the LORD their God and made for themselves two idols cast in the shape of calves, and an Asherah pole. They bowed down to all

the starry hosts, and they worshiped Baal. They sacrificed their sons and daughters in the fire. They practiced divination and sorcery and sold themselves to do evil in the eyes of the LORD, provoking him to anger. (2 Kings 17:16-17)

God specifically named and anointed Assyria to be an instrument of judgment on Israel. However, Assyria became arrogant under the blessing of God to judge Israel. God then promised and later executed his judgment upon Assyria found in Isaiah 10:5-19 and the book of Nahum.

God strengthened the southern kingdom to remain more faithful before the LORD for the sake of his promise to all of humanity. Many from the north fled to the south for protection from Assyria. In the midst of distress, they returned to the Lord.

However, because the Israelites were chosen by God for a special redemptive role, God held them to a greater standard of accountability and brought devastating judgment to cut off sin more quickly than other nations. In 586 BC, they too were taken into captivity for 70 years and Jerusalem was destroyed. God told us why:

Surely these things happened to Judah according to the LORD's command, in order to remove them from his presence because of the sins of Manasseh and all he had done, including the shedding of innocent blood. For he had filled Jerusalem with innocent blood and the LORD was not willing to forgive. (2 Kings 24:3-4)

In this case, it was growing idolatry and bloodshed brought on by the corruption of justice that brought the judgment of God in the form of Babylonian captivity. Most nations that are carried off into captivity cease to exist as a nation within a generation unless they are reunited with their homeland.

In Jerusalem's case, God raised up other nations to bring judgment and discipline upon his chosen people. It was God who inspired and empowered Nebuchadnezzar to conquer much of the Middle East. The prophet Jeremiah wrote:

With my great power and outstretched arm I made the earth and its people and the animals that are on it, and I give it to anyone I please. Now I will hand all your countries over to my servant Nebuchadnezzar king of Babylon. I will make even the wild animals subject to him. (Jeremiah 27:5-6)

In a theologically scandalous turn of events, God sided with Nebuchadnezzar. However, just as in Assyria's case, Nebuchadnezzar became excessively proud and God directly disciplined him as found in Daniel 4:27.

King Nebuchadnezzar came to his senses and acknowledged that heaven reigned. However, his son did not and arrogantly misused the articles from the God of all the earth to worship his false idols. By this time, the handwriting was on the wall and the judgment of God fell on the king of Babylon. In one night, Persia took over the entire empire of Babylon as a judgment upon the leadership of Babylon.

God himself had announced that he was going to raise up a man named Cyrus who would set Israel free:

This is what the LORD says to his anointed, to Cyrus, whose right hand I take hold of to subdue nations before him and to strip kings of their armor, to open doors before him so that gates will not be shut: I will go before you and will level the mountains; I will break down gates of bronze and cut through bars of iron. I will give you the treasures of darkness, riches stored in secret places, so that you may know that I am the LORD, the God of Israel who summons you by name. (Isaiah 45:1-3)

God had judged Israel for wickedness and idolatry by raising up Babylon. However, the King of Babylon became proud and sin increased in the Babylonian Kingdom so God then raised up the Persians. Eventually, the cycle would repeat itself with Greece and Rome.

God instituted government for the sake of fellowship. The few governmental leaders throughout history who sought to do righteousness and justice before God brought joy to heaven. They were like an oasis of righteousness in the midst of a desert of sin and oppressive government.

Over and over again justice was denied on the earth. Over and over again, the cries of the oppressed reached the ears of the righteous judge. Again and again, the righteous judge wept as judgment devastated the oppressor nations. Was there a way to end the cycle of sin and oppression leading to destruction?

Discussion questions

1. Describe serving under a leader. What made for good leadership verses bad leadership?

2. Describe a time when you had responsibility as a leader. What were some of the difficulties you faced in leading others that caused you to cry out for help?

3. Why do you think God still entrusted people to execute justice (including his judgments) when humanity is deeply affected by sin?

4. Genesis 9 basically says that the sanctity of human life in is the cornerstone of human government. Why is this so important? What do you think would happen if we made human suffering and ending poverty the primary foundation of justice instead of the eternal value of human life (as many humanists want to do)?

5. What role do you think repentance and dependence of God have on practicing justice?

Chapter 6:

The anguish of the Judge

"The most obscene symbol in human history is the Cross; yet in its ugliness it remains the most eloquent testimony to human dignity."
— R.C. Sproul

It had been a while since Caring Christian had visited. Wise Willie was becoming concerned for his friend. The spring snowstorm in the area had delayed the start of Caring Christian's new construction job. Meanwhile, Wise Willie had become busy with activities related to Lent and Passover. Suddenly, the doorbell rang and Wise Willie answered the door. Standing before him was a man who hadn't shaved, and looked stressed.

"You look like you've been through a war." Wise Willie said.

"Some shot," said Caring Christian. "When I got that shot for India, the pain went away after a day or so. The pain of this shot seems to go on and on and on!"

"Have you forgiven Swindler Sam," asked Wise Willie. "The Bible is really clear that we must forgive those who have hurt us."

"Forgive him-after what he did to me? Sam's swindling has ruined my life! I'm now behind on my mortgage payments for the first time in my life. Creditors are calling me every single day and my wife is in tears over it. She yelled at me last night because of the stress of the finances. Forgiving him means letting him off the hook. Meanwhile, I'm left with the bitter and painful circumstances. Forgiving him will not pay my bills. Forgiving him will not get me work," cried Caring Christian.

"You are right. Sometimes forgiveness is very costly," said Wise Willie. "Yet God delights in showing mercy to you and even to Swindler Sam if he will repent."

"God delights in showing mercy", grunted Caring Christian. "What mercy? If God is merciful, why did God allow me to experience so much trouble?"

"Sometimes, even the expressions of God's mercy are very painful", said Caring Christian with a concerned look. "Since it is around Lent, many Christians around the world are meditating on what Jesus did at the cross. How much have you thought about what Jesus did to bring you into his kingdom? The same scars at the cross still mark Jesus according to those who have seen him."

"You've always helped me before, Wise Willie. Since I trust, you, I'll go ahead and do it even though I do not feel like doing so. If God is so merciful, I still want to obey Jesus. Yet there are no tangible signs of his mercy."

With that, Wise Willie and Caring Christian prayed and Caring Christian gruffly declared forgiveness on Swindler Sam and the city. On Wise Willie's suggestion, Caring Christian also let go of bitterness against God for allowing the whole mess to begin with. Tears began to flow from Caring Christian as Wise Willie prayed for Caring Christian regarding the very difficult situation he was now facing.

"How are you feeling now?" asked, Wise Willie.

"I still feel awful", said Caring Christian. "It seems like it did not work. I still have bills to pay and a family that is mad at me- for what Swindler Sam did."

"Forgiveness is instantaneous but the affects are often delayed, it is like putting hydrogen peroxide on a wound. It will stop the infection of bitterness from killing your relationship with God and with other people. However, sometimes, the wounding takes time and effort to heal. Until the wound is healed, you must continue to forgive. By declaring war against bitterness and forgiving Swindler Sam, heaven will surely take note" said Wise Willie."

Just then Caring Christian's cell phone rang.

"I've got to go." said Caring Christian. "This had better work."

And with that, Caring Christian stormed off.

The joy of that first Sabbath:

On the surface, the story is pretty simple: God commands Israel to observe the Sabbath day and keep it Holy (Exodus 20:8-11). Jesus and his disciples are walking through the grain field on the Sabbath. They get hungry and begin picking (and then eating) the grain in the field. The religious leaders get all upset because they are "harvesting grain" (into their stomach) on the Sabbath. Jesus then rebukes them in word and then in action by healing a man on the Sabbath in front of on-lookers.

The religious leaders of Jesus day were really up-tight about this- attempting to earn God's approval. Meanwhile, it's now clear that the religious authorities were clueless. So what's with the commandment to remember the Sabbath day?

Genesis 1 described the creation of the heavens and the earth: Jesus spoke out what was in the heart of God the Father and at the sound of his voice, God the Holy Spirit acted in power. Creation came forth in its entire splendor. Job 38 described the angels staring at this spectacle of creation with singing and shouts of joy. Day after day, creation brought new demonstrations of the majesty and goodness of God.

However, all of this was leading up to the crowning moment of physical creation- that sixth day when God created man in his image. Like a grand party, God prepared all of physical creation for man-but there was still anticipation-like a groom anticipating seeing his bride in her bridal gowns. What would the first people do in seeing God's face and his creation?

We need to ask, "Why did God bless that seventh day and make it holy?" Initially, Scripture is vague about what happened on that 7th day. It simply says,

By the seventh day, God had finished the work he had been doing; so that on the seventh day he rested from all his work. And God blessed the seventh day and made it holy, because on it he rested from all the work of creating that he had done. (Genesis 2:2-3).

Something so special happened on that day between God and man that God treasured it forever. The kingdom of Heaven described this moment in Hebrews 4 as God's Sabbath rest. We can only imagine that first day when man and God openly rejoiced and loved each other without the presence of sin, shame, or darkness.

Even the disaster in the garden described in Genesis 3 could not drown out the joy of that first day. God promised restoration and redemption. While the serpent would strike the heel in apparent victory, God proclaimed a day when the seed of the woman will crush the serpent's head.

God delights in showing mercy

From that very first day in the Garden after man became entangled in sin, God began revealing his mercy and compassion. Instead of leaving Adam and Eve naked, the scripture says that God clothed them as a sign that redemption was possible-even as he escorted them out of the garden. Later, the prophet Micah would declare:

Who is a God like you, who pardons sin and forgives the transgression of the remnant of his inheritance? You do not stay angry forever but delight to show mercy. (Micah 7:18)

God is not like us who begrudgingly shows mercy. God is slow to anger and delights in showing compassion and kindness. God suffers long for the joy of showing mercy in response to repentance. Meanwhile, the prophet Isaiah announced:

Let the wicked forsake his way and the evil man his thoughts. Let him turn to the LORD, and he will have mercy on him, and to our God, for he will freely pardon. For my thoughts are not your thoughts neither are your ways my ways," declares the LORD. (Isaiah 55:7-8)

It brings the heart of God pleasure to show mercy and kindness to people-if they would just turn back to him. However, in many cases, the people would not turn back to him until devastating judgment is God's only option to show mercy.

Even in the midst of the most severe judgments, God always offered a merciful alternative. Before God flooded the earth in Genesis 6-8, God told Noah and he built the Ark. He was a preacher of righteousness for 120 years and others could have also built arks had they humbled themselves and given ear to God's instructions. In the midst of devastation in the cities of the plain, God spared Zoar. The blood of the Passover Lamb was painted over the doorposts preventing the angel of death from killing the first-born of Israel. Rahab's scarlet cord marked a safe-house in the midst of the destruction of Jericho. She told her friends and family who could have told others.

Even as the judgment foretold by Jeremiah and Isaiah was falling on Israel in the form of the nation of Babylon, God offered life instead of death. God repeatedly instructed Israel to surrender to Babylon and accept the captivity as his discipline-and many did, saving their lives. He was pleading with the people to turn back to the Lord through his prophetic messengers:

Therefore, O house of Israel, I will judge you, each one according to his ways, declares the Sovereign LORD. Repent! Turn away from all your offenses; then sin will not be your downfall. Rid yourselves of all the offenses you have committed, and get a new heart and a new spirit. Why will you die, O house of Israel? For I take no pleasure in the death of anyone, declares the Sovereign LORD. Repent and live! (Ezekiel 18:30-32)

Even up until the last possible moment, God was pleading with Israel and offering a merciful alternative to eternal destruction and death. Oppression and slavery were the consequences of national, corporate idolatry. While going to captivity, the prophets continued to proclaim the need to return to the Lord.

As a generation faces the storm of judgments surrounding the return of Jesus Christ to the earth, God has a mercy strategy. From the biblical prophets and modern prophetic voices, God once again proclaims a merciful alternative:

Rend your heart and not your garments. Return to the LORD your God, for he is gracious and compassionate, slow to anger and abounding in love, and he relents from sending calamity. Who knows? He may turn and have pity and leave behind a blessing- grain offerings and drink offerings for the LORD your God. (Joel 2:13-14)

Seek the LORD, all you humble of the land, you who do what he commands. Seek righteousness, seek humility; perhaps you will be sheltered on the day of the LORD's anger. (Zephaniah 2:3)

In the midst of destructive intervention to exalt righteousness, God continues to offer the alternative mercy strategy through repentance, humility, and seeking righteousness all the way to the very end.

Such is the anguish in the heart of judge when there is no alternative except to bring judgment that brings great pain, sorrow, and grief to many people. Yet Job in the midst of great affliction prophesied:

I know my Redeemer lives, and that in the end he will stand upon the earth. And after my skin has been destroyed, yet in my flesh I will see God; I myself will see him with my own eyes-I, and not another. How my heart yearns within me! (Job 19:25-27)

There was apparently no answer to the scourge of sin and then death in humanity- yet men and women of faith believed God would some how intervene. Was there a remedy?

Wanted: Who could stand in the gap?
From the beginning, God made known his desire to show his mercy and goodness instead of his anger in devastating temporal judgment. In the midst of the threat of judgment, God cried out through Ezekiel:

I looked for a man among them who would build up the wall and stand before me in the gap on behalf of the land so I would not have to destroy it, but I found none. (Ezekiel 22:30)

Before God's heavenly court-room, satan and his evil entourage demanded judgment and destruction against Israel. Yet, there were often a few people who lived uprightly before God who made covenant by sacrifice

(Psalm 50:5) for the sake of God's dream within their generation. In every case of mercy, God had found at least one person to "stand in the gap" on behalf of Israel and other people.

Throughout biblical history, If God found just a few qualified, upright people to stand in the gap and plead for mercy, destructive temporal judgments could be postponed or turned away. Abraham stood in the gap on behalf of Abimelech of Egypt in Genesis 20 and God healed Abimelech and his officials. Moses pleaded for mercy on behalf of the children of Israel after the golden calf incident. Scripture says:

At Horeb, they made a calf and worshiped an idol cast from metal. They exchanged their Glory for an image of a bull which eats grass. They forgot the God who saved them, who had done great things in Egypt, miracles in the land of Ham and awesome deeds by the Red Sea. So he said he would destroy them-had not Moses, his chosen one, stood in the breach before him to keep his wrath from destroying them. (Psalm 106:19-23)

God found Rizpah who stood in the gap on behalf of the land in David's time. Nineveh repented at the preaching of Jonah and God postponed destruction of the Assyrian Empire for another generation. Daniel as an intercessor stood in the gap for the return of Israel. Perhaps the people would repent so that judgment would be completely averted or at least the impacts minimized.

However, in the days of Jeremiah and Ezekiel there was no one who qualified to stand in the heavenly counsel of the LORD (according to Psalm 24:3-6) and plead for mercy on behalf of the nation. The sin of the nation was too great and gaps too many for simply a few people to turn away God's extremely painful redemptive discipline. Therefore Israel went into captivity. Yet God gave the nation intercessors to illustrate the need to fill the ultimate breach related to human offense against God.

Jesus, the judge of all the earth, repeatedly wept over those perishing through his prophetic friends. Humanity was doomed on a self-centered trajectory down to destruction. Even the most penitent and humble on the earth up to that time could not solve the problem of sin and the sentence of eternal justice and wrath hung over them. No one could repair the breach of fellowship inherited from Adam and Eve in Genesis 3.

The wrath of God over scorned love and every unrighteousness act could not be satisfied without an infinite penalty for each and every sin. The righteousness and justice of God demanded an eternal accounting for every single sin. There could be no true atonement or forgiveness of sin except through the shedding of innocent blood. God's painful interventions and even direct judgments could only slow the descent towards destruction and put road-blocks in the way of the path to eternal agony as the ultimate consequence and maturity of sin.

So great was God's heart-ache over our waywardness and so great was his desire for us to be restored to the fullness of joy. What God would do to solve the problem was both scandalous and awe-striking before heaven and earth. Scripture tells us what Jesus would do next:

In the beginning was the Word, and the Word was with God, and the Word was God. He was with God in the beginning. (John 1:1-2)

The Word became flesh and made his dwelling among us. We have seen his glory, the glory of the One and Only, who came from the Father, full of grace and truth. (John 1:14)

Being God and creator, Jesus has eternal privileges. He could have rested in the perfect eternal fellowship with the Father and the Holy Spirit without pain or pressure. Yet, more than His divine rights, position, and heavenly honor, he wants *you.*

Jesus the man of sorrows and faithful High Priest

Born of Mary, scripture does not talk a lot about how Jesus grew up. However, Jesus lived like every other man on the earth with certain human desires. This means that Jesus got hungry. Jesus also got physically tired like everyone else did. Joseph, the man everyone believed fathered Jesus, was a carpenter. Often the son would go to work as part of the father's trade and continue the father's business. Jesus understood the pain of being fatherless for part of his life as Joseph was not mentioned as alive in the midst of Jesus' ministry.

All the Bible says is that Jesus grew in favor with God and people. Once Jesus began his ministry, others took notice:

Isn't this the carpenter's son? Isn't his mother's name Mary, and aren't his brothers James, Joseph, Simon and Judas? Aren't all his sisters with us? Where then did this man get all these things? (Matthew 13:55-56)

Jesus grew up with siblings in obscurity like many of you have grown up with. In many cases, it meant sibling rivalry and the resulting bitter envy.

James, the brother of Jesus gives more insight on why Jesus may not have allowed many of the stories of his childhood to be included in the Bible:

Remember this: Whoever turns a sinner from the error of his way will save him from death and cover a multitude of sins. (James 5:20)

If James, the brother of Jesus was like everyone else, he probably sinned against his older brother Jesus many times-while Jesus did not sin against him. Jesus as the eldest brother (and knowing he is the Son of Man) was probably blessed as the "star" of the family. There was probably bitter envy because James and his younger brothers were blamed whenever anything went wrong as Mary knew from the angel who Jesus was.

As Jesus walked the earth, demons trembled and fled confessing that Jesus is the Son of God. Meanwhile, the full identity of Jesus remained hidden to human flesh. Isaiah prophesied:

Who has believed our message and to whom has the arm of the LORD been revealed? He grew up before him like a tender shoot, and like a root out of dry ground. He had no beauty or majesty to attract us to him, nothing in his appearance that we should desire him. He was despised and rejected by men, a man of sorrows, and familiar with suffering. Like one from whom men hide their faces he was despised and we esteemed him not. (Isaiah 53:1-3)

While fully God, Jesus lived on earth as if he were only fully human. Jesus only did what he saw the Father doing. All the miracles were done under through anointing of the Holy Spirit like every other man- not because Jesus was also fully God and using his "Divine Rights".

Like every other human being, Jesus was tempted in every possible way and stood the test in every possible way:

During the days of Jesus' life on earth, he offered up prayers and petitions with loud cries and tears to the one who could save him from death, and he was heard because of his reverent submission. Although he was a son, he learned obedience from what he suffered and, once made perfect, he became the source of eternal salvation for all who obey him and was designated by God to be high priest in the order of Melchizedek. (Hebrews 5:7-10)

With the powerful ministry and popularity came temptation to misuse the power for selfish gain. Popular opinion of the day called for the Messiah to raise up an army and overthrow the Romans using the sword and supernatural power like Joshua conquered the land of Canaan. Jesus resisted the popular messianic expectations and refused to be crowned king on the terms of prevailing opinion. The religious leaders criticized him and plotted to kill him- yet Jesus always answered with incredible wisdom with the Spirit of God upon him.

The terrible suffering of Jesus in the garden

On that awesome and terrible evening, his friends and disciples could tell something was wrong-but could not understand. The disciples were all pre-occupied with their own coming greatness and the Passover celebration in the midst of the coming battle. Jesus broke the bread and passed the cup instituting something new. Surely this was the last meal before the great revolution Jesus would lead propelling them into power and greatness. Jesus had their greatness in mind, but it was nothing like the disciples could have ever imagined.

Upon leaving the room and going into the garden Jesus finally took Peter, James, and John aside. Perhaps his three closest friends would understand:

Then he said to them, "My soul is overwhelmed with sorrow to the point of death. Stay here and keep watch with me." (Matthew 26:38)

Yet when he came to his friends later, he found them asleep.

Weeping in prayer, Jesus as a human being begged the Father to change what he was about to go through. Scripture records his words:

"My Father, if it is possible, may this cup be taken from me. Yet not as I will but as you will." (Matthew 26:39)

Through the darkness and the pain of that night, the humanity of Jesus was manifest. Luke's account tells us sweat poured down from his face because of his distress followed by blood as he wrestled with God through the night in prayer.

His closest friends had failed to offer support and comfort. Jesus already knew that one of them betrayed him. Another one would deny ever even knowing him. Why should he sacrifice all for them? The cup of human communion was going to be replaced with the cup of wrath.

Meanwhile, at his word, the angelic hosts could come and rescue him and his divine righteousness would be revealed. Yet there would be no way for humanity to be reconciled to God. All of Adam's descendents would perish in the fullness of their sin. What if his sacrifice was forgotten? This would make the sacrifice on the cross completely irrelevant. He would suffer in agony for nothing and all of humanity would be lost to eternal destruction.

In the midst of the bitter agony of that moment, the lingering smell of perfume brought back memories: There were still those who walked the earth who would risk it all for him; their future, their security, their dignity, and life itself. Jesus continued to wrestle. What would he do? Could the eternal prophesies be changed? Matthew records,

"He went away a second time and prayed, "My Father, if it is not possible for this cup to be taken away unless I drink it, may your will be done." (Matthew 26:42)

Finally, the decision was resolved in his heart. Jesus would do it for the sake of one. Jesus as the Good Shepherd would leave the 99 for the sake of one.

Let us fix our eyes on Jesus, the author and perfecter of our faith, who for the joy set before him endured the cross, scorning its shame, and sat down at the right hand of the throne of God. (Hebrews 12:2)

He would go through with the eternal plan for the sake of the woman and her seed-even if it only meant one person would understand, repent, and receive the free gift.

In the distance were torches and a commotion. As the crowds approached, more than one of his disciples drew his sword ready to fight. Surely this was the battle that would begin a great revolution. Yet Jesus ordered his disciples to stand down. Resolute, Jesus faced his disciples and the crowd saying,

But this has taken place that the writings of the prophets might be fulfilled. (Matthew 26:56)

Jesus was arrested, but not before convincing the Romans to let his disciples go. Stunned at the turn of events-and that Jesus did not fight, his disciples ran away terrified.

Like a lamb led to the slaughter:
Jesus was led bound and harassed before the Sanhedrin for a "trial". In the midst of the trial and bringing the witnesses against Jesus, they could not get two witnesses to agree on a charge against Jesus. Often the accusers would contradict each other though Jesus had a public witness with signs, wonders, and miracles.

Finally, two false witnesses came forward, putting his identity on trial. Only the Messiah had the right to tear down the temple and raise it up. The high priest then charged Jesus under oath to reveal his identity: *Are you the Christ?* Left with no choice, we read:

"Yes, it is as you say," Jesus replied. "But I say to all of you: In the future you will see the Son of Man sitting at the right hand of the Mighty One and coming with the clouds of heaven." (Matthew 26:64)

At this, the high priest tore his robes. Out of the bitter rage and envy, they found him guilty and deserving of death. What followed was more verbal abuse, insults, punches, slaps, and mocking of Jesus. *If you are the Son of Man, prove it!* Meanwhile, at any time, Jesus could have called millions of angels and ended the abuse and suffering.

Rejected by his own government and people, they sent Jesus on to Pilate. Pontius Pilate was used to intimidating others with the threat of crucifixion, humiliation, and a horrible death. Undoubtedly, Pilate enjoyed watching rebels sweat, squirm, and beg for mercy as he wielded his authority. He would then pronounce judgment and enjoy the cries of agony as the rebels were dragged away to experience public torture and death from crucifixion.

As Jesus was brought to trial, he simply stood there. Pilate knew that Jesus was handed over to him because of the bitter envy of the Jews. Instead of squirming and crying for mercy, Jesus simply stood there silent. Agitated and perhaps intimidated, Pontius Pilate asked, "What is truth?" As Jesus stood there silently, no one in history got such a profound answer. Was Jesus on trial, or was Pontius Pilate?

Meanwhile, the crowds were becoming agitated on Passover. Expectations were high. Many believed Jesus was the Messiah that would lead Israel to triumph over the Romans. The Messiah was supposed to have the Romans in chains. Meanwhile, Jesus stood before the Romans in chains- what?! Heartbroken and angry, the crowds cried out: *Crucify him!* In response to the healing and compassion, came scorned love, betrayal, and rejection.

Surely he took up our infirmities and carried our sorrows, yet we considered him stricken by God, smitten by him, and afflicted. (Isaiah 53:4)

Deprived of sleep, thirsty due to sweating and blood loss, and in emotional agony, the physical and emotional pain was only beginning.

After the sentence of crucifixion, Jesus was further beaten, punched, and mocked by the Roman Soldiers. A crown of thorns was twisted around his head. The thorns cut deep into his scalp and even into his eyes.

The scripture simply says that Jesus was flogged- but it was much more than just a few bad spankings, or even the crack of a bull-whip. The Romans use a special whip made of shards of bone, rocks, and other sharp objects. In hitting the victim, these shards would get imbedded in their skin. In pulling the whip away, the shards would shred their skin and deeper tissue.

Depicted accurately in *The Passion of Christ,* flesh and blood went flying as the victim screamed in agony.

But he was pierced for our transgressions, he was crushed for our iniquities; the punishment that brought us peace was upon him, and by his wounds we are healed. (Isaiah 53:5)

Over and over, the whip came down- back, legs, arms, and even his front side. Over and over the whip was ripped away, flesh, blood, and tissue flying to screams of agony.

Jesus was then led away to be crucified. Wearing crown of thorns piercing his scalp and eyes, bruised, and raw from head to toe, Jesus was led to Golgotha. Carrying the cross upon his ripped open back, his blood flowed through the streets of Jerusalem. In the horrible chaos there was the fragrance of that anointing several days ago deep in tattered skin, beard, and hair: some would still give it all for the sake of loving him.

The Crucifixion and culmination of suffering:

Finally, Jesus and the Roman guard reached the place of the skull. Refusing the anesthetic wine and vinegar, Jesus was laid on the cross, tied with ropes as the Roman soldiers reached for a nail. With the first blow, the nail pierced skin and shattered the main nerve in Jesus' arm sending searing pain throughout his body. From the right and left extremities of his body, searing pain swept through every nerve as both hands and then feet were nailed to the cross. As the cross was lifted up virtually every joint in Jesus' body became dislocated.

Making the pain worse were the tears of his mother Mary and John the beloved. All hope of the Messianic kingdom seemed lost for them. Meanwhile, with every blow and scream of agony, the religious leaders celebrated and jeered. Struggling to breathe, Jesus cried out:

Father, forgive them, for they do not know what they are doing. (Luke 23:34)

Before heaven and earth Jesus made intercession for us. His clothes were divided and the Roman Soldiers cast lots for them. A sign, advertising their crimes, was put on top of the cross to increase the humiliation. For Jesus it was: JESUS KING OF THE JEWS (Matthew 27:37).

Jesus did not die immediately after being nailed to the cross. For the next six hours, Jesus struggled to breathe. With every breath, agonizing pain swept through every nerve in his arms and feet. With every breath, his ripped-open back and legs rubbed against the rough timber inducing further injury and more searing pain. Exposed to the sun, heat, cold, and wind, sweat and blood poured out upon the ground. Thorns pierced his scalp and eyes. Bruised and beaten so badly, passerby's mocked because they could not recognize him.

We all, like sheep, have gone astray, each of us has turned to his own way; and the LORD has laid on him the iniquity of us all. (Isaiah 53:6)

As the day wore on, the physical pain and emotional suffering continued to increase. With one word, Jesus could have found relief. With one word, Jesus could have called the angels to come and stop this mockery of God's righteousness and majesty. That serpent shouted through the vocal chords of the religious leaders and bystanders:

Those who passed by hurled insults at him, shaking their heads and saying, "You who were going to destroy the temple and build it in three days, save yourself! Come down from the cross, if you are the Son of God! (Matthew 27:39-40)

Yet that "one word" never came.

In the midst of the agonizing events up until now, Jesus was still in joyous communion with the Father and the Holy Spirit. At noon, suddenly the sky went dark. Jesus cried out in agony:

About the ninth hour Jesus cried out in a loud voice, "Eloi, Eloi, lama sabachthani?"-which means, "My God, My God, why have you forsaken me?" (Matthew 27:46)

From eternity past nothing like this had ever happened: All of the sin and the wrath of God that we deserved were laid upon Jesus.

Anger is cruel and fury is overwhelming, but who can stand before jealousy? (Proverbs 27:4)

For the first and only time in eternity, joyous eternal fellowship between Father, Son, and Holy Spirit was disrupted. With more loud cries, Jesus gave up his spirit.

It was finished. Every great and terrible prophetic scripture related to Jesus' suffering and death found its fulfillment. Jesus would suffer for our sake to stand in the gap to renew covenant possibility. Jesus the righteous Judge would rather take the judgment of God for us instead giving us over to the sin and the consequences you and I deserved. He died of a broken heart because *he* wanted you reconciled to God.

Discussion questions:

1. Why do you think God requires Christians to forgive (even horrible things such as sexual abuse or other forms severe exploitation) as a prerequisite to being forgiven?

2. Why is the Sabbath so special to God?

3. Why do you think God delights in showing mercy towards people?

4. Jesus "stood in the gap" and continues to make intercession for us. (Romans 8:24) What do you think the role of intercession is in the New Testament?

5. We looked at the suffering of Jesus on the cross- what does this say about the sanctity and value of human life?

Chapter 7:

The joy of the Judge

"I would not give one moment of heaven for all the joy and riches of the world, even if it lasted for thousands and thousands of years." - Martin Luther

Wise Willie heard the door bell ring. Caring Christian had not left his house happy. Surely, he was probably offended at what he said in their last visit. He had seen Caring Christian with his family at church that morning from a distance before he got called to help with a mechanical problem at church. Surprised, Wise Willie came to open the door to find Caring Christian.

"I feel closer to Jesus than ever!" said Caring Christian.

"What happened?" asked Wise Willie as his countenance brightened.

"Pastor preached about how God can make all things work together for the good. He preached about how God allowed David to be mistreated to expose terrible things in his own heart. God has been exposing terrible things in my own heart and in the heart of my family through this ordeal. At the end of the service, my whole family came up to repent and God floored us!" We wept, we laughed, and we shouted for joy."

"What do you mean that God floored you?" asked Wise Willie:

"I felt the joy of the Lord over me like can never be fully described. After understanding better what Jesus went through on the cross for me, who I am to Jesus, the joy I've brought to his heart in attempting to follow him and can bring to his heart, and my family's eternal destiny he purchased; we are beside ourselves."

Caring Christian continued: "My family lost $50,000 but, we are now sure that God will take care of us. We now love God and each other more than ever and we have a joy better than money can buy."

Justice served- The Joy of vindication

Caring Christian barely experienced the edges of the joy of the LORD over our salvation and fellowship with him. This was the edge of the joy that was set before Jesus as he went to the cross. David prophesied of this great joy:

I said to the LORD, "You are my Lord, apart from you I have no good thing." As for the saints who are in the land, they are the glorious ones in whom is all my delight. (Psalm 16:2-3)

Throughout history God has had his loyal ones who would sacrifice for the sake of the dreams in his heart. There was Abraham who left everything and forsook the gods of his fathers for the sake of the LORD and a land he did not know. Moses left the comforts of Egypt behind for the sake of his people. David didn't care about being king as much as he desired a time when God's glory (and blessing) would rest upon Israel in righteousness fulfilling of all the promises the LORD had made. Daniel risked his life to intercede for the remnant of God's people, Israel. Mary of Bethany put her life and livelihood at risk in an extravagant act of worship to Jesus.

Yet because of Adam's sin that affected the entire human race, even his most loyal ones could not live with the LORD forever in heaven. Every lie, every act of theft, every movement of bitter hatred, every deed of unrighteousness and every act of disobedience against the infinite God of justice demanded the eternal death penalty of retribution (Romans 6:23). Without the shedding of blood, there was no forgiveness of sin. The gulf of sin was far too wide for anyone to bridge.

Yet more than righteous vengeance due to our sin, God wanted reconciliation and redemption for us. Speaking of the kingdom of heaven, Jesus said:

The kingdom of heaven is like a treasure hidden in a field, when a man found it, he hid it again, and then in his joy went and sold all he had and bought that field. (Matthew 13:44)

Again, the kingdom of heaven is like a merchant looking for fine pearls. When he found one of great value, he went away and sold everything he had and bought it. (Matthew 13:45)

Many people only partially interpret these Bible passages. We typically think that we are the seekers looking for something good. Many times these passages are taught as if we are the ones giving up everything to find the kingdom of God. We find something good when we find the kingdom of heaven and count the cost. This is true, but this is less than half of the real interpretation.

In reality, God sought us first, so that we could seek him. In these parables, Jesus is the great seeker of treasure. Jesus is the merchant looking for the pearls. Jesus redeemed the sea and the fields of humanity who said a collective "no" for the sake of even one person who would say "yes" to love and fellowship with God forever. After Jesus gave up his spirit, scripture gives us glimpses of what happened:

"When he ascended on high, he led captives in his train and gave gifts to men" (Ephesians 4:8)

Death could not hold Jesus down. The grave could not stop God from reconciling those who loved him. Jesus took back the keys of death and Hades. Satan no longer controlled human destiny. Eternal judgment had fallen: Paid in full!

When the LORD brought back the captives to Zion, we were like men who dreamed. Our mouths were filled with laughter, our tongues with songs of joy. Then it was said among the nations, "The LORD has done great things for them." The LORD has done great things for us, and we are filled with joy. (Psalm 126:1-3)

The penalty of sin could no longer prevent his faithful ones from coming to him. People like Abraham, Isaac, Jacob, Joseph, Moses, David, Daniel, and many others shouted for joy as Jesus broke open the way to the Eternal Zion. One day, heaven and earth will be completely joined together as God makes his home with people.

Before Jesus came to earth and died, God had set up a system of blood sacrifice for Israel to practically demonstrate the awesome consequences of sin. Those who acted in faith through the blood sacrifices looked forward to a day when God would do something to atone for sin. Year after year, decade after decade for centuries, sacrifices were offered in faith. However, the blood of lambs, bulls, and goats could not remove the terrible consequences of sin.

At the death and resurrection of Jesus, all of those animal sacrifices done in faith were now redeemed. God justified those who trusted in him and declared their sin forgiven when Jesus died. Those who had died in faith could now enter the direct presence of God because their sin had been atoned for and Jesus led them home. The resurrection of Jesus and the empty tomb is open evidence before heaven and earth of God's pleasure to bring justice by canceling the debt of sin.

Justice served: the joy of eternal reconciliation

Jesus broke open the way for the prodigals like all of us, to come home. The parables of Luke 15 (parable of the lost sheep, parable of the lost coin) hint at the great joy in heaven over reconciliation. Jesus says:

In the same way there will be more rejoicing in heaven over one sinner who repents than over ninety-nine righteous persons who do not need to repent. (Luke 15:7)

In the same way, I tell you, there is rejoicing in the presence of the angels of God over one sinner who repents. (Luke 15:10)

Father, Son, and Holy Spirit rejoice at the exaltation of righteousness on the earth. Heaven celebrates the righteousness of God vindicated in Christ Jesus. The angels celebrate one more snatched from the jaws of eternal destruction. Father, Son, and Holy Spirit rejoice that one more has been reconciled to heaven.

Our own hearts can rejoice again as we discover that God's wisdom is indeed superior to the wisdom of the serpent in producing joy, peace, and pleasure. Mercy still triumphs over judgment in the heart of Jesus. If you have never been reconciled to God, this is the moment everything can change.

How can I be reconciled to God?

Perhaps as you have been reading this, you realized that you do no know God. Or perhaps you realized that your relationship with God has been completely broken because you've been living for yourself, bitter at God.

We were never designed to live alienated from God. However, Jesus told Nicodemus that everyone must be born again in John 3:1-8 to enter the kingdom of God. Jesus was referring to a promise written the prophets:

"This is the covenant that I will make with the house of Israel after that time", declares the LORD. "I will put my law in their minds and write it on their hearts. I will be their God, and they will be my people. No longer will a man teach is neighbor, or a man his brother, saying, 'Know the LORD', because they will all know me, from the least of them to the greatest," declares the LORD. "For I will forgive their wickedness and will remember their sins no more." (Jeremiah 31:33-34)

I will give you a new heart and put a new spirit in you; I will remove from you your heart of stone and give you a heart of flesh. And I will put my Spirit in you and move you to follow my decrees and be careful to keep my laws. (Ezekiel 36:26-27)

Jesus then told Nicodemus why he had come to earth.

For God so loved the world that he gave his one and only Son, that whoever believes in him shall not perish but have eternal life. (John 3:16)

While we could do nothing to save ourselves from our self-centered sinful death-spiral, God directly intervened. As partially described in chapter 6, Jesus suffered and died on the cross so that eternal justice could be done. His great suffering is the measure of his great love for us and his hatred of evil along with what sin does to people.

However, we must do something that God has enabled us to do: We must make a choice to turn to Jesus and turn away from the things that displease God such as bitterness, (that can lead to murder), sexual immorality, selfishness at other people's expense, and lying:

"Everyone who confesses the name of the LORD must turn away from wickedness." (2 Timothy 2:19)

"Everyone who calls on the name of the LORD will be saved. (Romans 10:13).

Even as Jesus picked up the cross because of the eternal joy set before him, he invites us to do the same thing: turn away from everything displeasing to God and turn to Jesus and never look back. Here is an example of how you can do it now:

God, I come to you in great need. I turn away from every act of hatred, theft, sexual immorality, and deception. I want no other gods except you Jesus. I choose to forgive everyone who hurt me. Forgive me Jesus, be Lord of my life and save me. Thank you for dying on the cross to take the judgment for my sin. I want to live your resurrection life and love you with all my heart, soul, mind, and strength.

If you just did this for the first time, or are giving your life back to Jesus, everything has changed.

Even from the beginning, God offered Adam and every human being a choice: life with Jesus or death. Jesus renewed this choice for all of us.

Then Jesus said to his disciples, "If anyone would come after me, he must deny himself and take up his cross and follow me. For whoever wants to save his life will lose it, but whoever loses his life for me will find it. What good will it be for a man if he gains the whole world, yet forfeits his soul? Or what can a man give in exchange for his soul? (Matthew 16:24-26)

We must all make a choice- are we going to live for ourselves or are we going to live for Jesus on his terms (who deeply values others)?

Like Adam in the garden, we must daily make the choice: life or death. We can live our own life, or exchange our life to walk like Jesus did- in humility, righteousness, and justice. Now that we are in the kingdom, we must make the choice to live for him daily.

From sons of perdition to sons of God;

Most of the Church does not understand the night and day difference following Jesus means. Turning away from sin and turning to Jesus changes EVERYTHING including our eternal destiny. Scripture says that before we turned to Jesus we were sons of perdition; destined to experience the fullness of sin we were choosing along with the consequences of eternal destruction earlier described. Scripture says:

All of us also lived among them at one time, gratifying the cravings of our sinful nature and following its desires and thoughts. Like the rest, we were by nature objects of wrath. But because of his great love for us, God, who is rich in mercy, made us alive in Christ even when wee were dead in transgressions-it is by grace you have been saved. And God raised us up with Christ and seated us with him in the heavenly realms in Christ Jesus, in order that in the coming ages he might show the incomparable riches of his grace, expressed in his kindness to us in Christ Jesus. (Ephesians 2:3-7)

Yet to all who received him, to those who believed in his name, he gave the right to become children of God- (John 1:12)

In turning to Jesus and away from sin, our identity has changed. God's Holy Spirit dwells within us as promised by the prophets of old.

Your identity has just changed-but you may or may not feel different. Faith is not dependent upon whether we feel anything special. Faith is all about trust. Jesus surely did not "feel" like going through the suffering and death at the cross- yet as a man he trusted God. Our faith is dependent upon the trustworthiness of what Jesus did on the cross for us, recorded in scripture without error.

Yet there is no such thing as faith without action. Scripture is now clear that we are to verify our new identity through water baptism:

Whoever believes and is baptized will be saved, but whoever does not believe will be condemned (Mark 16:16).

In him you were also circumcised, in the putting off of the sinful nature, not with circumcision done by the hands of men but with the circumcision done by Christ, having been buried with him in baptism and raised with him through your faith in the power of God, who raised him from the dead. (Colossians 2:11-12)

Water baptism is a clear sign of obedience and verifying your identity before heaven and earth as a son of God, an heir to the kingdom forever.

When we gave surrendered our lives to Jesus, the Holy Spirit came to live inside our hearts. For many generations before Jesus, the prophets promised the day when the Holy Spirit would come and dwell within people and move their hearts into fellowship with God. Jesus promised the Holy Spirit to guide, and teach us. He promised the Holy Spirit to help us and comfort us from within. Since the day of Pentecost, the Holy Spirit is now available to everyone.

Before Jesus ascended into heaven, Jesus gave the marvelous promise of the Holy Spirit.

But you will receive power when the Holy Spirit comes on you; and you will be my witnesses in Jerusalem, and all Judea and Samaria, and to the ends of the earth. (Acts 1:8)

The same Spirit that empowered Jesus to live godly and do signs and wonders in obedience to the Father lives in us. Paul said,

I have been crucified with Christ and I no longer live, but Christ lives in me. The life I live in the body, I live by faith in the Son of God, who loved me and gave himself for me. (Galatians 2:20)

As sons of God, part of our inheritance includes doing the works of Jesus- healing the sick, raising the dead, authority over demons, and power to live like Jesus. That same Holy Spirit wants to immerse us in power to live like Jesus when he walked the earth.

We are now citizens of heaven- we are representatives of the kingdom of heaven. Heaven is a glorious place and a kingdom. However, this kingdom is very different than the culture and values of this world. Heaven is now our home because judgment has been released on our behalf through the cross of Jesus.

What is heaven on earth going to be like?

With the change of our eternal identity came a change of our eternal destiny. A growing number of people have had experiences of going to heaven and meeting Jesus. They come back wide-eyed and filled with joy without being able to describe the colors, sounds, and other experiences. Many of them echo what the apostle Paul said:

However it is written: "No eye has seen, no ear has heard, no mind has conceived what God has prepared for those who love him"- but God has revealed it to us by his Spirit. The Spirit searches all things, even the deep things of God. (1 Corinthians 2:9-10)

The apostle John, when he saw only a little bit about what God had planned for his beloved ones fell down to worship messenger. The angel who was showing him all of this told him to stop (Revelation 22:9-10).

Jesus spent more time warning about hell than talking about heaven. I believe that God purposely did not tell us much. God wanted our imaginations under the anointing of the Holy Spirit to go wild with what was possible in fellowship with God:

Finally, brothers, whatever is true, what ever is noble, whatever is right, whatever is pure, whatever is lovely, whatever is admirable-if anything is excellent or praiseworthy-think about such things. (Philippians 4:8)

In thinking and trying to imagine what life will be with Jesus, the fountain of life and righteous pleasure, we end up building our mind and hearts up for the present. When our hearts and minds are filled with heaven, we can better represent the kingdom of heaven in living on earth.

However, we are not left completely in the dark. The scriptures give inferences and hints about what life will be like when heaven and earth are fully joined together. We are blessed with desire for when God finally dwells unhindered with man.

Then I saw a new heaven and a new earth, for the first heaven and the first earth had passed away, and there was no longer any sea. I saw the Holy City, the new Jerusalem, coming down out of heaven from God, prepared as a bride beautifully dressed for her husband. And I heard a loud voice from the throne saying, "Now the dwelling of God is with men, and he will live with them. They will be his people, and God himself will be with them and be their God. He will wipe every tear from their eyes. There will be no more death or mourning or crying or pain, for the old order of things has passed away." (Revelation 21:1-4)

Life will be very different with Jesus for all eternity than our present experience is on the earth. We must use the time on earth to get ready. However, it is much easier to describe what will NOT be in heaven.

What is not in heaven:

The Bible says life will be different when heaven comes to earth. God Almighty will dwell among people. There will be no more sea or physical separation from loved ones.

In John's day, travel was very difficult and dangerous. It was something ultra-special when guests came in from out of town. Families were separated by distance and that distance often does damage to family relationships simply because of the difficulty of living in this age. In the eternal age, there will be no more geographical separation.

God promised there would be no more death. In this age, it appears that death has the final word and that life ends with loss and sadness. However, scripture declared otherwise:

When the perishable has been clothed with the imperishable, and the mortal with immortality, then the saying that is written will come true: "Death has been swallowed up in victory." "Where, O death, is your victory? Where, O death, is your sting?" (1 Corinthians 15:54-55)

When I saw him, I fell at his feet as though dead. Then he placed his right hand on me and said: "Do not be afraid. I am the First and the Last. I am the Living One; I was dead and behold I am alive for ever and ever! And I hold the keys of death and Hades." (Revelation 1:17-18)

Around the world, the greatest underlying fear every culture faced is death. Death was the gateway to unspeakable horror and torment without Jesus. However, with the death and resurrection of Jesus, everything changed.

In heaven, there is no more sorrow or pain-or anything that causes sorrow and pain. No more physical injuries such as bruises or broken bones. No more physical infirmities such as Diabetes, Muscular Dystrophy, ALS, skin irritation, or Leprosy. There is no more blindness or deafness in heaven.

There will be no more heart attacks, cancer, or strokes. There will be no more physical deformities such as blindness or deafness or missing limbs. The blind will see, the deaf will hear, and the lame will be able to leap for joy. No more destructive viruses, bacteria, or other microscopic organisms to cause sickness and pain.

No more sorrow and pain also means no more emotional and mental defects. There will be no schizophrenia, ADHD, Autism, or any other mental disorders that cause great pain and difficulty. There will be no anxiety disorders and clinical depression. In our own person, we will have resurrected bodies and renewed minds.

Our environment will no longer be hostile. No more snake bites, dog bites, insect bites, or *When Animals Attack* videos made as creation will be at peace. No more destructive earthquakes, floods, famines, poisoned water, and other natural disasters as creation will be set free from the curse of sin. There will be no more scorching heat or bitter cold as Jesus is our sun and shield.

The way we interact with each other will be different. No one with hatred or holding a bitter grudge against someone will be allowed into the kingdom. A bitter grudge is an idol of pride that must be cast down.

In many cases, we relate with each other as a product of our brokenness. There will be no more subtle manipulation or intimidation to get our own way. No more need to compete with each other for honor and pleasure because we will know the fountainhead of all pleasure and joy that satisfies us all. No more crime and no more sin. No more painful slander or cutting innuendos. No more painful toil because there will be no more curse. No more broken promises, hope deferred, or disappointment. Even the pain of regret will be swept away as he wipes away every tear from our eyes.

The people who love Jesus that we disagreed with will be deep companions forever, swept up in the goodness of God. There will be no more pain from rejection.

When we stand on the sapphire sea before the throne, there will be no more dirty secrets to hide. There will be no more humiliation or fear of humiliation because there will be nothing left to hide. Everything to know about us will be known-and yet love covers a multitude of sin, brokenness, and shame. Seeing how Jesus honored us in our broken humanity and what we were saved from, even the least in the kingdom of heaven will rejoice in honoring and serving others.

Without the horrors of eternal death, suffering, sorrow, and pain as the foundation of debilitating fear, it also means that there will be no more fear in heaven as we stand in awe of God's majesty and kindness. On earth, we have no idea how much emotional and physical energy we spend worrying. Even the scripture says:

There is no fear in love. But perfect love drives out fear because fear has to do with punishment. The one who fears is not made perfect in love. (1 John 4:18)

In heaven, there will be no more fear in the presence of perfect love. With perfect love will come perfect peace and security in Christ.

The promise of resurrection bodies

When Jesus rose from the dead, he broke the power of death forever. When Jesus met with his disciples, he had an incorruptible body that would never die again. He ate fish with the disciples on the seashore. He talked with his disciples. People recognized and distinguished Jesus from other people.

However, with a resurrection, incorruptible body, Jesus did some strange things. Jesus walked on water effortlessly. Jesus also walked through walls and ascended out of view before his disciples. He broke the bread with the disciples on the road to Emmaus and then disappeared. Other people in the Bible reported strange supernatural experiences such as teleporting from one place to another.

Our current physical bodies could never contain the eternal joy and glory God has prepared for us. Moses wanted to see the glory of God, but God warned him:

"But", He said, "you cannot see my face, for no one may see me and live". (Exodus 33:20)

Scripture tells us that even physical mountains melt at the presence of God, how much more would weak (sinful) human flesh?

Jesus promised a resurrection for everyone. Some will rise to face every consequence for this sin leading to everlasting disgrace and torment. They will go from the temporary imprisonment and severe distress in Hades into the lake of fire to experience the fullness of the sin they chose and suffer in both soul and body.

For those who are redeemed by Jesus, the resurrection is something they have looked forward to. The redeemed throughout human history will rise to experience eternal glory beyond anything we can imagine. Even for those who "barely made it in" without eternal rewards, our physical bodies will be greatly enhanced.

First, we will be able to recognize each other. We will not be an amorphous blob in heaven. The disciples were able to recognize the face of Jesus in his resurrection body. Some who have had glimpses of heaven tell of recognizing loved ones who died. Others recognized great men of the Old and New Testament. We will get to know each other and hear their stories.

Second, the Bible tells us that we will have no more physical pain in our bodies or disabilities. We will be able to see and hear with much greater clarity. Even people with the best vision or hearing on earth in this age will look disabled compared to what we will have in forever in our resurrection bodies. We will be able to taste and smell the goodness of God. We will be able to touch and interact with the physical realm and the spiritual realm simultaneously.

Third, we will have eternal stamina- our physical bodies will no longer get tired or need food and water to survive. Eating and drinking will be one of the great pleasures we get to enjoy with each other. There is no waste in heaven. A greater stamina without physical fatigue or pain will give us a greater ability to serve and honor God, other people, and then the rest of creation.

We will have much greater physical abilities in our resurrection bodies than what we currently have. We will be stronger and faster than we were in our natural bodies. There will be no more separation from the ones we loved on earth and new friends who love Jesus in heaven. Yet our physical abilities and the glory in our resurrection bodies will clearly differentiate according to what is decided at the judgment seat of Christ (1 Corinthians 15:40-42).

Forth, we will have much greater emotional and mental capacities to enjoy God and each other with for all eternity. There will be no more "mental bugs" where we forgot important details or facts. We will be able to communicate verbally and non-verbally with clarity. The great mysteries of the faith will no longer be mysterious. The languages of the world will no longer be a hindrance but a blessing as the effects of the tower of Babel will be undone.

Scripture indicates that Adam and Eve had incredible mental and spiritual powers before the fall in the garden. They were able to see God directly and live. They were able to interact with the physical and spiritual realms simultaneously. There were no barriers to communicating with the animals and the rest of creation. There was possibly the ability to travel at the speed of thought. Hollywood's depiction of "superpowers" may reflect what people once had before sin entered the picture.

These abilities and more will be restored to varying degrees at the judgment seat of Christ when we get our new resurrected bodies. Our capacity to enjoy God and impart life and blessing to others through our incorruptible bodies will also vary based on the findings at the judgment seat of Christ. We will need the blessing of resurrection bodies to enjoy the culture of heaven for all of eternity.

The culture of heaven

The culture of heaven is radically different than the cultural norms of the earth. In heaven, the character and nature of God sets the cultural norms for all. We will understand the courage, humility, and sacrifice of Jesus. In exalting Jesus, the same courage, humility, and sacrifice for righteousness will be honored in others as well. In seeking the severity and the kindness of God, we will all likely weep with both sorrow and joy when we meet him.

Scripture is deliberately vague about what we will do in heaven on earth. However our interaction with God forever will begin with him wiping every tear away from our eyes. The prophets foretold of us knowing our God:

They will be my people, and I will be their God. I will give them singleness of heart and action, so that they will always fear me for their own good and the good of their children after them. I will make an everlasting covenant with them. <u>I will never stop doing good to them</u>, and I will inspire them to fear me, so that they will never turn away from me. I will rejoice in doing them good and will assuredly plant them in this land with all my heart and soul (Jeremiah 32:38-41).

Your love, O LORD, reaches to the heavens, your faithfulness to the skies. Your righteousness is like the mighty mountains, your justice like the great deep. O LORD, you preserve both man and beast. How priceless is your unfailing love! Both high and low among men find refuge in the shadow of your wings. They feast on the abundance of your house; you give them drink from your river of delights. For with you is the fountain of life; in your light we see light. (Psalm 36:5-9)

With endless wonder, we will finally see what the prophets of the Hebraic and Greek scriptures described before falling on their faces awestruck.

Far beyond the greatest shows on earth, we will behold the source of all beauty and majesty, God himself. Like little children, the sense of joy and the wonder of discovery will be fully restored in gazing at God. Those who encountered the throne of God saw lightning, fire, a sea of glass, an emerald rainbow, elders bowing down, the four living creatures, and radiant light coming from the One who sat upon the throne. Absolute glory, absolute purity, absolute peace and joy in his presence forevermore are our inheritance-and it just gets better.

This incredibly awesome and beautiful God is forever humble. Jesus was and is still the God who kneels. We will finally see Jesus for who he really is-and stand in awe of his righteousness, kindness, and humility. We will also get to understand how deeply Jesus actually suffered to bring us atonement, reconciliation, and eternal glory.

With Jesus the servant as the fountainhead of righteous joy, peace, and pleasure- serving and imparting life to others will be one of our greatest delights. There will be no more curse, pain, or toil to steal the joy of serving others honoring others, and learning from others throughout human history. We will learn the fullness of what Jesus meant when he said, "It is more blessed to give than receive."

Overwhelmed at the goodness and mercy of God, we will get to serve each other and have fellowship with others throughout human history. Scripture describes the kingdom of heaven as the wedding feast of the Lamb. The world's best feasts with the most elegant and noble settings are but a shadow the beauty, the elegance, and pleasure of feasting at that final wedding feast. We will finally get to see Jesus drink the fruit of the vine again in fulfillment of his promise to us:

Then he took the cup, gave thanks and offered it to them saying, "Drink from it, all of you. This is my blood of the covenant, which is poured out for many for the forgiveness of sins. I tell you, I will not drink of this fruit of the vine from now on until that day when I drink of it anew with you in my Father's Kingdom." (Matthew 26:27-29)

We will get to share the joy of the Lord and celebrate forever what God has done for us to bring us into the kingdom. We won't compete to be the greatest. We will see the greatness of Jesus as Alpha and Omega- the beginning of all and end-all and chief desire.

With humanity finally in right relationship with God, everything under human authority delegated by God will finally be set right. Scripture says that we will be an extension of the rule of God forever. The increase of his government, there will be no end. We will never need to end our worship to God but we will rejoice with singing and dancing, draw near in intimacy, and fall on our faces in awe of God forever. We get to rejoice in honoring each other and loving each other forever as well.

In this age, all enjoyable things inevitably come to an end on the earth. The wedding celebration ends because everyone is tired out from celebrating. The honeymoon ends and people go back to work after all the money is spent. The grand fireworks and laser light show fizzles because there is nothing more to burn. However, God has an endless supply of resources-indeed he is our source. Indeed, the psalmist wrote:

You have made known to me the path of life; you will fill me with joy in your presence, with eternal pleasures at your right hand. (Psalm 16:11)

In the presence of God, love will never end but become greater throughout the ages. Peace will never end. The joy will never end or decrease but go on increasing forever. It will take all of eternity to simply begin to understand the endless expressions of kindness and joy from God.

The joy of heaven wants to touch earth in this age.

The disciples had just returned from a recent successful ministry trip where they saw the wonders of God in their midst in Luke 10. Jesus said that he saw satan fall like lightning. The judgments of God in heaven pushed the kingdom of darkness back on earth. The disciples saw the joy in the hearts of the people they served. His disciples returned in Luke 11 asking Jesus how to pray. Jesus repeated what he said in Matthew 6:

Our Father in heaven, hallowed be your name, your kingdom come, your will be done on earth as it is in heaven. (Matthew 6:9-10)

Heaven is described as a place where there is no sorrow, pain, or death. While heaven and earth will not be brought fully together until Jesus comes back to rule from Zion on earth, we are commissioned to bring people small glimpses of heaven to the earth.

When Jesus began his ministry on earth, scripture tells us what happened: The blind could see, the deaf could suddenly hear, paralytics were walking. Every disease known to man was blown away by the goodness of God. Even the dead were raised. Isaiah prophesied of this glorious day:

The Spirit of the Sovereign LORD is on me because the LORD has anointed me to preach good news to the poor. He has sent me to bind up the brokenhearted, to proclaim freedom for the captives and release from darkness for the prisoners, to proclaim the year of the LORD's favor and the day of vengeance of our God, to comfort all who mourn, and provide for those who grieve in Zion- to bestow on them a crown of beauty instead of ashes, the oil of gladness instead of mourning, and a garment of praise instead of a spirit of despair. They will be called oaks of righteousness, a planting of the LORD for the display of his splendor. (Isaiah 61:1-3)

The healing miracles of Jesus were simply a preview and testimony of a kingdom where there is no more suffering, death, crying, or pain. Among the poor and the oppressed, there was suddenly great joy and hope as heaven touched earth. Heaven's justice was breaking in, turning mourning into dancing. With great joy, Jesus executed judgment against sickness, disease, and drove out demons that were oppressing the people. Even death could not stand in his presence.

In the midst of the gloom and painful oppression, the kingdom of God was breaking in. Jesus' message was simple:

"Repent, for the kingdom of heaven is near." (Matthew 4:17)

The call to repentance was a call to turn from sin. The call of repentance was an invitation to be part of something far better than anything we can imagine. Jesus was willing to deeply offend people so that they could hear the eternal gospel and not miss out on the coming glory and joy of his kingdom. We are called to re-present Jesus in words and deeds.

Anointed to bring the justice of Heaven on the earth

In chapter 5, God entrusted much of his justice system on the earth to people. After his death and resurrection, Jesus commissioned his disciples saying:

"All authority in heaven and on earth has been given to me. Therefore go and make disciples of all nations, baptizing them in the name of the Father and of the Son and of the Holy Spirit, and teaching them to obey everything I have commanded you. And surely I am with you always, to the very end of the age." (Matthew 28:18-20)

With his words, Jesus sent his apostles to bring joy to heaven to earth through proclaiming the eternal gospel, healing the sick, raising the dead, and casting out demons (Mark 16:16-20). David had prophesied of this day:

For the LORD takes delight in his people; he crowns the humble with salvation. Let the saints rejoice in this honor and sing for joy on their beds. May the praise of God be in their mouths and a double-edged sword in their hands, to inflict vengeance on the nations and punishment on the peoples, to bind their kings with fetters, their nobles with shackles of iron, to carry out

the sentence written against them. This is the glory of
all his saints. Praise the LORD. (Psalm 149:4-9)

While corrupt rulers still rule the earth, David prophesied of a called-out and wholehearted people seated with Christ in the heavenly places who would rule over the evil kings of the earth and their demonic conspirators through prayer. Jesus is the just judge but will he find faith on the earth?

The kingdom of God has come and is coming. Heaven's justice and joy is invading earth's corruption and sorrow. Heaven and earth were meant to come together, beginning in the hearts and the works of those who are whole-heartedly loyal to Jesus.

Jesus is looking for trustworthy people who will bring the joy of heaven's justice to earth against sin, oppression, disease, and sorrow. Jesus as fully man could not physically be everywhere at one time while he walked the earth. Jesus commissioned his disciples to bring the gospel of the kingdom to every ethnic group. In the midst of Jesus' ministry, Matthew recorded:

When he saw the crowds, he had compassion on them, because they were harassed and helpless, like sheep without a shepherd. Then he said to his disciples, "The harvest is plentiful but the workers are few. Ask the Lord of the harvest, therefore, to send out workers into his harvest field." (Matthew 9:36-38)

The great commission includes a cry from the heart of God to bring justice to the poor beginning with physical relief. Heaven wants to break in with justice to bring joy on the earth in the midst of great sorrow. God promised the Holy Spirit to all believers. Jesus promised that because of the Holy Spirit, we could do what Jesus did as a human on the earth- and even greater works than those. Heaven is coming to make every wrong thing on the earth right.

Chief among what is on God's heart are the poor of the earth. Many are willing to go out for the sake of those who can give us something back. Very few are willing to go into the harvest fields for the sake of those who cannot give us anything back in the natural. Natural wisdom says that since there is a limited amount of resources available, if we spend ourselves on behalf of the poor, we will end up with nothing and poor ourselves.

The economies of the world are based upon the need to allocate scarce resources. With only limited amounts of resources, the focus is on buying and selling. The ones who accumulate the most resources legally "win" according to worldly economic wisdom. Wealth is defined as the ability to control lots of people and resources.

Yet heaven's wisdom trumps worldly wisdom- including God's economic system. Instead of limited resources, God is the source of unlimited supply of everything needed to demonstrate righteousness and justice. There are unlimited resources from heaven to display the righteousness, kindness, and mercy of God to everyone. Heaven's economy is based upon giving and receiving. Having wealth in heaven is defined by those who can give and bless others in the greatest ways.

What do you suppose might happen if God's people practiced heaven's economy in the midst of a dark and painful world? God repeatedly spoke of his compassion for the poor and broken-hearted in the scriptures: Affection and desire for the people (even though they mistreat us because of the brokenness in their emotions, relationships, and bodies) and anger at the ongoing injustice occurring against them. God promised a blessing upon those who would bring the demonstration of the kingdom of God to them:

He who oppresses the poor shows contempt for their Maker, but whoever is kind to the needy honors God. (Proverbs 14:31)

He who is kind to the poor lends to the LORD, and he will reward him for what he has done. (Proverbs 19:17)

Then Jesus said to his host, "When you give a luncheon or dinner, do not invite your friends, your brothers or relatives or your rich neighbors. If you do, they may invite you back and so you will be repaid. But when you give a banquet, invite the poor, the crippled, the lame, the blind, and you will be blessed. Although they cannot repay you, you will be repaid at the resurrection of the righteous." (Luke 14:12-14)

How the church and society treats the poor and the needy is a litmus test: Do we really believe God's word related to the value of life? Do we really believe Jesus will use us to bring a little bit of heaven to the suffering and broken on earth? Jesus wants to bring the joy of heaven's justice to the poor through us. The kingdom of God is at hand.

Discussion questions:

1. Describe how you think loving mercy for the sake of others can be an expression of perfect justice for Jesus. What does it look like practically?

2. What do you look forward to in heaven the most?

3. What do you think would happen on earth if our relationships and activities imitated heaven?

4. What do you think heavenly justice released on the earth looks like?

Chapter 8:

The Judge who rewards

"My goal is GOD HIMSELF. Not joy, not peace, not even blessing but HIMSELF...my GOD."- Leonard Ravenhill

The door bell rang and Wise Willie got up to answer. Outside, Caring Christian was waiting dressed in a suit and tie, holding a briefcase with a big grin on his face. Wise Willie opened the door.

"Did you hear the news? Swindler Sam has been caught and it looks like I may get back some of the money he swindled from me." Caring Christian continued, "I guess God worked this whole mess out to my good to bring me and my family closer to him. I now know a lot more about the heart motivations of Jesus the judge. Meanwhile I did not lose anything in the long-term.

With tears, Swindler Sam has asked to meet with me again. I don't want to see his family ruined. I just want Swindler Sam to stop swindling. Maybe God will change his name to Sorrowful Saved Sam."

"I'm glad God redeemed the whole mess for you", said Wise Willie. "In the meantime, you learned some incredibly valuable lessons about how to handle your life affairs. By the way, why are you so dressed up?"

"I need to get ready for a very important meeting with the judge, the district attorneys, and with Swindler Sam later today", said Caring Christian. "The best possible thing that could happen is that Swindler Sam turns to Jesus and stops swindling people."

"Can I tell you a little bit about another very important meeting with the judge in your future? Without understanding the judgment seat of Christ, your understanding of Jesus the judge will not be complete."

Wise Willie continued, "Regardless of the outcome of your court case on earth, you are already victorious before the eyes of Jesus, the eternal judge. You overcame bitterness. Instead of growing bitter, you forgave Swindler Sam and prayed for his welfare. Under your leadership, your family loves Jesus much more deeply than ever before. You've learned to trust God more and he has been providing for your family. God will reward you forever."

"WHAT?" A shocked Caring Christian yelled. "After all those expressions of pain, tears of sorrow, and feeble attempts to honor Jesus, God will reward me forever for *this*? I've never heard anything about this. I need to understand this more."

The exaltation of God's justice

Caring Christian has gone through a whirlwind of emotions in experiencing the heart of the judge. Beginning with some presumptuous over-confidence, Caring Christian did not understand the heart of Jesus as a judge. When God's temporal judgment (discipline) fell on his life to prevent destructive sin from growing and the result was anger, pain, and heart-ache. However, even then Caring Christian could sense the goodness of God at work to bring healing and redemption in his life. Suddenly Caring Christian's life is now far deeper in God as the restoration of his heart and life is even better than before.

We've also taken a journey into the emotions and heart of Jesus the judge. God is filled with humility and joy in the midst of the fellowship of Father, Son, and Holy Spirit. God delights to exalt righteousness and His righteous wisdom. Jesus also desires humanity to enter into the glory of fellowshipping with the Trinitarian God.

When humanity rejected and scorned Jesus' offer of goodness and mercy, his anger was roused out of heartache and hurt. Sin has a deceptive, cancerous effect on humanity, dragging people into the perdition that they unwittingly chose for themselves. God need not act in wrath and anger- sin would simply grow and lead to ultimate destruction, unending torment, and pain. Indeed, we need God's continued intervention to deliver us from evil (no matter how painful or disruptive it is).

Unlike the angels whom sinned out of arrogant pride, Adam sinned because of unbelief. God did not leave us to our own devices but continued to pursue redemption for us. Like a doctor treating malignant cancer, God prescribed the painful treatments to arrest cancer until his solution came forth in the fullness of time. Made in his image, God in his desire for us placed painful roadblock after roadblock to our obstinate highway to hell that sin was taking us on.

In the midst of even the most severe judgments, a merciful alternative was always offered. God wept tears of heartache and pain over the people hurt because of his temporal judgments and discipline meant to save us.

The ache in God's heart over his wayward children and what they suffered (and what they would suffer) is so great that before time, God knew he would do something. Jesus the righteous judge would enter his own story to take the judgment we deserved on himself at the cross. Justice would be done by Jesus on behalf of us.

Where is justice for Jesus? As fully God, Jesus has his inheritance in fellowship with the Father and the Holy Spirit. He does not need people to be completely satisfied. Yet as fully man, Jesus has not received his inheritance on earth. Justice has not been done.

Indeed, the Holy Spirit will raise up a cry that was in the Moravians under Count Zinsendorf: *Give the Lamb the reward of His suffering!* Jesus as a man, is not ruling and reigning as king over Jerusalem-and he will not come back until his own brothers, the Jewish people invite him back (Matthew 23:37). Only one generation will crown Jesus as the rightful king as he returns to earth. However, we have an opportunity to live in a way that is worthy of a king, where justice and love is satisfied.

Justice for us: the judgment seat of Christ-

For those who continue to trust Jesus in word and deed, the question where we will spend eternity has been settled at the cross. Jesus released judgment at the cross to break open the way for man to be reconciled to God through His blood. God changed our destiny from eternal destruction, torment, and agony through the fullness of sin under his wrath in the lake of fire to eternal righteousness peace, and joy his kingdom forever. Our place in heaven is secure as we continue to faithfully follow Jesus forward.

However, much is still undecided even for a believer. Life is like the 100-yard dash to the finish to determine the gold medal in the Olympic Games. Athletes train for their whole lives for less than ten seconds that determine who gets glory, honor, riches, and fame on earth. Life on earth in this age is like that 100-yard dash that determines whether we get glory, honor, and riches in the eyes of heaven for all of eternity.

The scripture will not be broken. All will die and be subjected to the judgment (Hebrews 9:27) except for the generation that welcomes Jesus back to the earth as the judge of the living and the dead. Yet even they will be evaluated on that glorious day. As believers, we are all still subjected to judgment:

So we make it our goal to please him, whether we are at home in the body or away from it. For we must all appear before the judgment seat of Christ, that each one may receive what is due him for the things done while in the body, whether good or bad. (2 Corinthians 5:9-10).

For those who have followed Jesus as Lord and Savior, there is no condemnation. Sin has been covered at the cross. The Greek word for "judgment seat" is *bema* which entails the possibility of eternal rewards.

Without the judgment seat of Christ for believers, there cannot be God's eternal justice for his beloved ones. For example, Jesus gave the parable of the talents: One guy he gave five talents to, another guy two and another guy only one. It would appear that God is "playing favorites" by giving one person five talents, the other person two and a third guy only one-unless there was an eternal accounting. The judgment seat of Christ is that eternal accounting.

Meanwhile, this is the same God who knelt to wash feet and who loves humility. In his great wisdom and knowledge, God deliberately gave some people more wealth, influence, and honor than others. God forces the man with only one talent to confront selfish pride (in the form of bitter envy and self-pity) to walk worthy of the kingdom of heaven. God forces the next guy with two talents to confront selfish pride in the form of bitter envy and vain conceit and entitlement. God then forces the final man with the most talents to confront selfish pride in the form of conceit, entitlement, complacency, and laziness.

Heaven does not evaluate our lives the way the systems of this world do. Our fallen humanity evaluates what we produced and what we did in determining what the "pecking order" is in society. Those who have five talents get a shot at all the glory and honor in this age. Those who have only one talent are consigned to supporting roles and experiencing the oppression of the people at the top; too bad.

Meanwhile, heaven evaluates us on "good", "faithful", and servant". The guy who was faithful with one talent and multiplied their talent 100-fold will be much more greatly rewarded than someone with more talents and was somewhat lazy and only multiplied it 30-fold. Paul understood this and prayed:

With this in mind, we constantly pray for you, that our God may count you worthy of his calling, and that by his power he may fulfill every good purpose of yours and every act prompted by your faith. We pray this so that the name of our Lord Jesus may be glorified in you, and you in him, according to the grace of our God and the Lord Jesus Christ. (2 Thessalonians 1:11-12)

Heaven's system of evaluation is much different than earth. Those who never had opportunity on earth to be great because of circumstances, lack of wealth, and relational dynamics still have opportunity to great forever. Ultimately, only heaven's opinion of our lives counts anyway. The judgment seat of Christ is the great equalizer for all eternity. Rich or poor, slave or free; God's justice will be exalted forever. We can all win the prize of Jesus as our exceedingly great reward.

Our greatest moment or, the most painful moment?

As followers of Jesus, we must prepare for that great and awesome day when we stand before him. After giving our lives to Jesus, this will be the most important appointment we have for all of eternity. For Paul his whole life vision was based upon the moment he would stand before Jesus. Paul repeatedly exhorted the Corinthian believers about this great and terrible day:

My conscience is clear, but that does not make me innocent. It is the Lord who judges me. Therefore judge nothing before the appointed time; wait until the Lord comes. He will bring to light what is hidden in darkness and will expose the motives of men's hearts. At that time each will receive his praise from God. (1 Corinthians 4:4-5)

For some, it will be a day of great joy and vindication. We don't have any idea of what Jesus feels or thinks for us when we resist bitterness and lust to practice righteousness in the midst of pain and difficulty. Some chose to love Jesus at great personal sacrifice-even to the point of death. Choices made that others mocked, ridiculed, and persecuted will be vindicated forever by Jesus. Paul wrote,

If any man builds on this foundation using gold, silver, costly stones, wood, hay or straw, his work will be shown for what it is, because the Day will bring it to light. It will be revealed with fire, and the fire will test the quality of each man's work. If what he has built survives, he will receive his reward. If it is burned up, he will suffer loss; he himself will be saved, but only as one escaping through the flames.
(1 Corinthians 3:12-15)

For many other believers, that day will be marked by tears of deep regret and sadness. Since they gave Jesus the leadership of their lives and trusted in his work on the cross, there is no condemnation. They will still experience the joy and peace of heaven forever. However, their life on earth will have been wasted-and there will be profound understanding that sin still has awful consequences.

God created us with the longing to be great forever. However, greatness in heaven's eyes is far different than on the earth. Jesus himself warned of a differentiation among those whom he would bring into the kingdom:

Anyone who breaks one of the least of these commandments and teaches others to do the same will be called least in the kingdom of heaven, but whoever practices and teaches these commands will be called great in the kingdom of heaven. (Matthew 5:19)

The apostle John gave insight on how to live in great expectancy and joy for that day:

And so we know and rely on the love God has for us. God is love. Whoever lives in love lives in God, and God in them. In this way, love is made complete among us so that we will have confidence on the day of judgment, because in this world we are like him. There is no fear in love. But perfect love drives out fear, because fear has to do with punishment. The one who fears is not made perfect in love. (1 John 4:16-18)

The structures of power and might on the earth in this present age evaluate us based on what we can do for them. Meanwhile, heaven measures what we have become: *How deeply did we become conformed into the likeness of Christ?*

A brief review of the culture of heaven...

In order to understand greatness in heaven forever, we need to understand the culture of the kingdom of heaven forever. It was for the joy of eternal fellowship with us that he endured infinite wrath and atoned for our sin. Through the prophets of the old and new testaments, God promised a day when there will be no more death, sorrow, pain, and mourning for his sons and daughters. There will be no lack of resources, beauty, or splendor in heaven. All these things will pass away.

Scripture promises that we will be resurrected from the death with brand new physical bodies. We will finally see things for what they really are. We currently see in a glass dimly and darkened but we will have completed understanding in that day. We will have new physical abilities and stamina that we can stand in the presence of

God. We will clearly understand the folly and horrors of sin that Jesus saved us from. We will also finally completely understand what Jesus went through to save us.

Out of this well of understanding of the kindness and severity of God will come an unending fountain of joy and gratitude. Those who chose Jesus will be ushered into a place of endless feasting, fellowship, and joy with Jesus Christ. It will be our great pleasure to worship God, honor each other, and lead by serving the rest of creation forever.

Suffering, pain, sorrow, and death are only temporary human realities in this age for those who love Jesus. However, with these difficult and painful realities are opportunities to love Jesus in extravagant fashion (from heaven's perspective). In the eternal ages to come, we will no longer have these opportunities.

For example, there will be no more hunger pains in our physical bodies and we will enjoy food whenever we desire in the eternal ages. However, there will be no more chances to suffer hunger pains through fasting with prayer for the sake of others as an extravagant act of worship to Jesus. No more opportunities to give sacrificially (and suffer lack on earth) for the sake of the gospel and other people as we will have access to endless resources to declare the manifold wisdom of God to all creation. There will be no more opportunities to suffer through toil (as there will be no more pain) for the sake of loving Jesus and other people.

There will be no more opportunity to do courageous acts of faith (because we cannot perceive and understand fully). We will all understand God's wisdom and ways perfectly. There will be no more "risky" acts of faith. We only have these opportunities in this age- in this short lifespan when we can only see into a mirror darkly.

What is exalted in heaven?

Our understanding of the wisdom and justice of God are clouded by this present evil age. However, this will not always be so. Paul wrote of that glorious day:

Now we see but a poor reflection as in a mirror; then we shall see face to face. Now I know in part; then I shall know fully, even as I am fully known.
(1 Corinthians 13:12)

When we are finally safe in the presence of God with resurrected bodies, we will finally have full understanding of his ways. We will understand the rightness of God's wisdom and justice in bringing superior pleasure and joy to all of creation. We will understand fully the folly of our sinful selfishness and pride and be disgusted at it. We will understand the suffering and sorrow Jesus went through on the earth to save us. Paul had glimpses of this understanding while on earth and exploded with desire:

I want to know Christ and the power of his resurrection and the fellowship of sharing in his sufferings, becoming like him in his death, and so, somehow, to attain to the resurrection from the dead. (Philippians 3:10-11)

Paul started his apostolic ministry as the least of the apostles in 1 Corinthians. As Paul grew further towards the likeness of Jesus he better understood the great gap between Jesus' perfections and himself. Paul called himself as the least of all the saints in the book of Ephesians. Finally, near the end of his life, Paul described himself as the chief of sinners as the glory of Christ shined even brighter into the eyes of his heart.

Indeed, God revealed himself to Abraham in the midst of difficulty. Hebrews 12 declared that God showed Abraham a city, an eternal destiny.

"Do not be afraid, Abram, I am your shield, your very great reward" (Genesis 15:1)

From Genesis to Revelation, Jesus revealed himself as the great prize, the reward:

"Behold, I am coming soon! My reward is with me, and I will give to everyone according to what he has done. (Revelation 22:12)

Paul, James, and other writers of scripture talk about the rewards of God as a huge motivator to overcome: John testified of overcoming pain and difficulty in releasing the justice of God:

Now have come the salvation and the power of the kingdom of our God, and the authority of his Christ. For the accuser of our brothers, who accuses them before our God day and night has been hurled down. They overcame him by the blood of the lamb and by the word of their testimony; they did not love their lives so much as to shrink back from death. (Revelation 12:10-11)

In the ages to come, we will no longer have the opportunity to overcome sorrow, pain, and difficulty. The opportunity to overcome is only in this short timeframe of life in this age. However, even as Jesus overcame and will be exalted as a man, it brings God pleasure to exalt his beloved ones, made in his image in righteousness and truth.

The glory of overcoming: brokenness redeemed

In the book of Revelation, Jesus spoke repeatedly of overcoming and eternal rewards to prepare the end-time Church for victory. Every insult, every unjust wound in our hearts we took because of Jesus, every bad circumstance, every beating, and ounce of persecution is an opportunity:

And we know that in all things God works for the good of those who love him, who have been called according to his purpose. For those God foreknew he also predestined to be conformed in the likeness of his son, that he might be the firstborn among many brothers. And those he predestined, he also called; those he called, he also justified; those he justified, he also glorified. (Romans 8:28-30)

When something negative comes against us (circumstances, demonic attack, or sinful actions of people), God takes it personally. He wants to release vengeance on the enemy of our souls who inspired the mess but is looking for friends who overcome.

Paul often spoke of the difficulty that he faced for the sake of the gospel. He confronted pain, sorrow, persecution, and many other difficulties for the sake of making Jesus known to people blinded by satan's tyranny. Paul gave us all a secret of God's justice when he wrote to the believers in Corinth:

Praise be to the God and Father of our Lord Jesus Christ, the Father of compassion and the God of all comfort, who comforts us in all our troubles, so that we can comfort those in any trouble with the comfort we ourselves have received from God. For just as the sufferings of Christ now overflow into our lives, so also through Christ our comfort overflows. (2 Corinthians 1:3-5)

The only way Paul could overcome was through knowing the comforter- the Holy Spirit in answer to prayer. It would have been easier to quit, but God's love in Paul compelled him forward. Love for Jesus and others drove him onward.

Under the grace of God he overcame through practicing righteousness and humility in dependence upon the Holy Spirit. In response, God rewarded him with authority to set people free and bring the comfort of the Holy Spirit to the broken. In the places where Paul was wounded and overcame, he became a vessel of God's mercy and justice to many other people. Meanwhile Paul will be forever rewarded by God and people for overcoming and releasing the blessing to people. Paul's joy will be off-the scale and so can ours through overcoming through Christ:

Each heart knows its own bitterness, and no one else can share its joy. (Proverbs 14:10)

Imagine every bitter pain getting reversed because we overcame. Imagine every heartache transformed by God into a channel of blessing for others. Every physical blow and depravation redeemed to be a channel of healing for the sake of others. Every incident of humiliation and shame now a source of joy and honor, overcome and transformed by the radiance of God's justice. This is what Jesus made possible- and wants to do for you.

Paul bragged like a fool through parts of Second Corinthians 11 and 12 of his sufferings because he understood the principle. God gave Paul authority as an apostle to bless and impart life because he overcame pain, sorrow, and difficulty. He wrote,

That is why, for Christ's sake, I delight in weaknesses, in insults, in hardships, in persecutions, in difficulties. For when I am weak, then I am strong. (2 Corinthians 12:10)

In the end, the trouble would be another channel to bring God's compassion to broken people and joyful justice for what Jesus did on the cross for you and me.

Meanwhile, Paul will be rewarded forever at the judgment seat of Christ for overcoming the pain and sorrow. Paul wrote his Corinthian friends:

For our light and momentary troubles are achieving for us an eternal weight of glory that far outweighs them all. So we fix our eyes not on what is seen, but on what is unseen. For what is seen is temporary, but what is unseen is eternal. (2 Corinthians 4:17-18)

At the end of his life, Paul was stuck in prison and most of his ministry partners had abandoned him. Execution at the hands of the Roman government loomed. Yet, he wrote to Timothy:

I have fought the good fight, I have finished the race, I have kept the faith. Now there is in store for me the crown of righteousness, which the Lord, the righteous Judge, will award to me on that day-and not only to me, but also to all who have longed for his appearing. (2 Timothy 4:7-8)

Paul's last words were not of despair, but of great joy and victory. Before Paul had made it to heaven, Jesus had assured him that he had won the crown. He had crowned the judge of all the earth with a life worthy of the King of Kings. Will we have a life of extravagant devotion to crown Jesus with great joy or will we only have the ashes of folly to present to a merciful savior?

The treasures of redemption:
Jesus exhorted the crowds to live for heavenly treasure, not treasure on the earth (Matthew 6:19-20). Jesus told more than one person to sell everything and pursue the heavenly treasure. Many of the treasures of heaven are not simply physical treasures. God deliberately hid things in plain view for us to search out (Proverbs 25:2-5). God spoke to Jeremiah:

"Call to me and I will answer you and tell you great and unsearchable things you do not know." (Jeremiah 33:3)

Jesus compared the Teachers of the Law who (through humbling themselves) became his disciples to owners who brought out the old and new treasures. Indeed in Christ are hidden all the treasures of wisdom and knowledge (Colossians 2:5). Paul counted everything as a loss compared to the all-surpassing greatness of knowing Jesus.

Some of these secret treasures from heaven are only shared in the context of deep intimacy with him. Jesus deliberately spoke in parables to stir up hunger to know God. The prophets of old were primarily friends with God, not ones who proclaimed a message. John the Baptist called himself a "friend of the bridegroom" (John 3:28-29).

The apostle John leaned into the heart of Jesus. John was also the only apostle to know who Jesus' betrayer was before that horrible night in Gethsemane.

The apostle John, Isaiah, Daniel, and others saw the beauty in God's sanctuary. According to John's account, the streets are made of pure gold. The gates are made of giant pearls. Every gemstone that is pleasing to the eye is part of the wall. The whole city is filled with life, beauty, and majesty radiating from the glory of God.

The greatest treasures of earth are dull compared to the beauty and majesty of Heaven. Yet the scriptures also describe things in this age of sorrow, pain, and suffering that will be saved for the ages to come. Compared to beauty of heaven, the things of this earth are dull and mundane. Yet they are considered treasures forever because of the One who values them as precious.

Scripture clearly indicates that there are books written about us in heaven. God showed the prophet Malachi:

Then those who feared the LORD talked with each other, and the LORD listened and heard. A scroll of remembrance was written in his presence concerning those who feared the LORD and honored his name. "They will be mine," says the LORD Almighty, "in the day when I make up my treasured possession. I will spare them, just as in compassion a man spares his son who serves him." (Malachi 3:16-17)

Of these acts of righteousness the writer of Hebrews said,

God is not unjust; he will not forget your work and the love you have shown him as you have helped his people and continue to help them. (Hebrews 6:10)

Every act of simple devotion to Jesus, every act of righteousness is recorded. Not one is missing.

For example, Jesus witnessed everyone putting their gifts into the offering, including a widow who threw in two small coins. Jesus said of this widow:

"I tell you the truth, this poor widow has put more into the treasury than all the others. They all gave out of their wealth; but she out of her poverty, put in everything-all she had to live on." (Mark 12:43-44)

There are some acts of extravagant devotion that so moved the heart of God, he made them publicly known as a memorial and example to us. Mary of Bethany's act in John 12 is a classic example. In another incident, the angel told Cornelius,

"Your prayers and gifts to the poor have come up as a memorial offering before God."(Acts 10:4)

God honored Cornelius as the first gentile to receive the gift of the Holy Spirit apart from physical circumcision, redefining the understanding and expression of "chosen people" in his day. It's all written in the book of remembrance because God's heart was so moved by his persistent devotion and loyalty.

Scripture indicates there are other treasures from this age that are saved by God forever. For example, scripture indicates that God saves our tears of love, intercession, and even repentance (Psalm 56:7-8). Scripture also indicates that God somehow collects the blood of the martyrs (Genesis 4:10-11; Revelation 6:9-11 etc). Surely, there are other treasures from this age that are preserved by God as well. Compared to the riches of the age to come, these objects will look bland. Yet like family heirlooms, they are treasured by all of heaven because people used these items in love and devotion and deeply blessed the heart of God.

Of course, the greatest treasures that are saved from this age are people. Jesus is the great treasure seeker and each one of us is the pearl of great price. We are God's workmanship; fearfully and wonderfully made for him forever. The angels declared of Jesus before the Father:

You are worthy, to take the scroll and to open its seals, because you were slain, and with your blood you purchased men for God from every tribe and language and people and nation. (Revelation 5:9)

Later, the angels declared:

"Amen! Praise and glory and wisdom and thanks and honor and power and strength be to our God for ever and ever. Amen!" (Revelation 7:12)

In beholding mere humans, redeemed by God from this age of sorrow and suffering, they can see and understand the great joy we will bring to the Father, Son, and Holy Spirit. In response the angelic hosts have erupted in joyous worship.

Grace upon Grace upon Grace

When we stand before Jesus, we will understand the grace of God with much greater clarity. God's grace inspired our acts of love and righteousness- beginning with our hearts turning from sin in repentance and to Jesus for salvation. God then empowered us by His grace to follow through in obedience. Paul understood this dynamic.

But by the grace of God I am what I am, and his grace to me was not without effect. No, I worked harder than all of them-yet not I, but the grace of God that was in me. (1 Corinthians 15:10).

As a final dimension of God's grace, God then answered and responded in overwhelming ways to give us greater grace. Why should Jesus reward us for anything we do? Jesus said,

"Suppose one of you had a servant plowing or looking after the sheep. Would he say to the servant when he comes in from the field, 'Come along now and sit down and eat'? Would he not rather say, 'Prepare my supper, get yourself ready and wait on me while eat and drink;

after that you may eat and drink?' Would he thank the servant because he did what he was told to do? So you also, when you have done everything you were told to do, should say, 'We are unworthy servants; we have only done our duty.'" (Luke 17:7-10)

Compared to the beauty, riches, and majesty of heaven, we are all unworthy servants. Even our most extravagant acts of devotion on earth cannot compete with the endless perfection of heaven's works.

David understood this dynamic in preparing to build a glorious dwelling place for God. As a final act of his kingship, David trained Solomon to lead, made alliances with foreign leaders, gave extravagantly towards the cost of building materials, and inspired the people to follow his lead in giving extravagantly as well. God responded by pouring out the joy of giving on the people. Overwhelmed with the joy of heaven that touched earth, David prayed,

"But who am I, and the people who are my people, that we should be able to give as generously as this? Everything comes from you and we have given you only what comes from your hand." (1 Chronicles 29:14)

God remembers David's devotion of his youth. God gave David a dream that his glory would rest in Zion when he was a despised shepherd boy. Jesus called himself "The Son of David" in honor of fulfilling David's dream. As a final gracious judgment related to this age, God fills us with joy and honor for acts of righteousness *as if we were the only ones who had done something worthy of honor.*

Eternal rewards: He will be worth it all
Out of the overwhelming grace and kindness towards us, Jesus promised incredible rewards for those who are faithful and kept his commandments to the very end. In Revelation 2-3, Jesus gave hints at the value of the eternal rewards that were promised to those who overcame because of love for Jesus and other people.

A crown of glory

God gave supernatural understanding to Paul that he had won the crown of glory. James wrote of this reward:

Blessed is the man who perseveres under trial, because when he has stood the test, he will receive the crown of life that God has promised to those who love him. (James 1:12)

In the ancient days, Greece and Rome also held the Olympic Games. The winner got a beautiful living wreath. They were given a place of honor in the city's citizenship and they were the talk of the town for days. That glorious moment would only last for a few days, but athletes trained their whole life for an opportunity to win the crown.

In contrast to that perishable wreath, Paul understood what winning the crown of glory from Jesus meant:

Do you not know that in a race all the runners run, but only one gets the prize? Run in such a way as to get the prize. Everyone who competes in the games goes into strict training. They do it to get a crown that will not last; but we do it to get a crown that will last forever. (1 Corinthians 9:24-25)

In the ancient games, only one person could win the crown. However, it is possible for anyone to win a crown from Jesus in exchange of a life lived worthy of the King of Kings. Jesus Christ wore a crown of thorns for our broken emotions and corrupt inner thought life (that influences our words and actions) so that we could perhaps wear a crown of glory forever.

Garments of righteousness and an eternal testimony of honor:

Jesus promised crowns of glory and so much more for those who overcome. In writing to the Church of Sardis (with a false reputation), he said:

Yet you have a few people in Sardis who have not soiled their clothes. They will walk with me, dressed in white, for they are worthy. He who overcomes will, like them, be dressed in white. I will never blot out his name from the book of life, but will acknowledge his name before my Father and his angels.
(Revelation 3:4-5)

Later we find in the book of Revelation that Jesus is leading the armies of heaven dressed in radiant white linen. The garments depicted acts of righteousness of the saints. Like in boy scouts, the military, and other professions, our clothing shows forth our accomplishments in Christ and acts of righteousness.

Most of these acts are small and "insignificant" in the eyes of people. Some were scorned by people. However, God has not forgotten anything done to love him and his people. Meanwhile, every sin we confessed and repented of will never be brought up by God at that judgment seat. The blood of Jesus covers our sin.

For those who overcome, Jesus will tell our story before the Father, the angels, and the saints. Scripture tells us that there are books written about our life (Exodus 32:32-33; Malachi 4:16; Revelation 20:12-15) As the Author and finisher of our faith, Jesus is writing a story. We will have a testimony of pain and difficulty that ends with great joy and honor that lasts forever. We will stand in awe as we see how Jesus finished our story to bring joy to the Father.

Meanwhile, we will see the one who wrote the story of our lives and what he did to save us. Branded a traitor, David had been stripped of royal honor and humiliated. David fled to the wilderness to escape King Saul. The Psalmist David wrote looking forward to that day:

Find rest, my soul, in God alone; my hope comes from him. He alone is my rock and my salvation; he is my fortress, I will not be shaken. My salvation and my honor depend on God; he is my mighty rock, my refuge. (Psalm 62:6-7)

Indeed, Jesus suffered jeers, mocking, and public humiliation at the cross so we could have a testimony of salvation and honor before God, the angels, redeemed humanity, and all of creation forever.

Glory and abilities in our resurrection bodies-
Foundational to Christianity is the resurrection from the dead. Jesus arose the dead- indeed death could not hold the man who said, "I am the resurrection and the life." The Old Testament prophets prophesied of the resurrection.

By faith, Abraham, when God tested him, offered Isaac as a sacrifice. He who received the promises was about to sacrifice his one and only son, even though God had said to him, "It is through Isaac that your offspring will be reckoned." Abraham reasoned that God could raise the dead, and figuratively speaking, he did receive Isaac back from death. (Hebrews 11:17-19)

Abraham prophesied of the resurrection through his actions. Job, David, Daniel, and others testified in the scriptures of the resurrection.
The glory of the resurrection is our great hope, our great dream. Death will not have the last word, but Jesus the way, the truth, and the life will! At the end, even death is cast into the lake of fire- destroyed forever.
Paul wrote to the Corinthian Church because of false doctrine concerning the resurrection from the dead. False teachers were bringing confusion into the church Paul planted saying that there was no resurrection from the dead. Paul countered in saying:

For since death came through a man, the resurrection of the dead comes also through a man. For as in Adam, all die, so in Christ all will be made alive. (1 Corinthians 15:21-22)

Every human being who has lived on the earth will be resurrected from the dead. Paul warned the Church in

Corinth to flee against sexual immorality as they were sinning against their own (resurrection) bodies. Indeed, the crown of life and glory in our resurrection bodies is related to overcoming the lusts of the flesh.

However, the resurrection from the dead will not be the same for everyone. For some it will be the worst moment of their life as they stand before God and give account. They are then sentenced to eternal torment in soul and physical agony in the lake of fire forever. Jesus said of one of them, that it would have been better for them to have not even been born (Matthew 26:24).

Even among the redeemed from all eternity, our resurrection bodies will differ in the glory according to our works. Paul said,

The sun has one kind of splendor, the moon another, and the stars another; and stars differs from star in splendor. So will it be with the resurrection from the dead. (1 Corinthians 15:41-42)

We who are redeemed will all have resurrection bodies that are free of suffering, pain, sorrow, and deficiencies. However, we will not all have the same splendor, glory, and honor in our resurrection bodies. Scripture is clear that some will have more glory and capacity to impart peace, joy, and life than others because of the way we overcame.

On the day we meet Jesus, we will understand what Jesus laid down and suffered in his physical body to walk on the earth. We will understand the physiological resistance Jesus overcame to walk blameless before God and man. We will behold his nail prints and better understand the ordeal Jesus went through for us. *Jesus suffered and died physically so I could have eternal glory and honor in my resurrection body.*

The exaltation of Jesus the Judge:
Revelation 2-3 describes many other rewards that Jesus promised for those who overcome. These rewards affect things such as our proximity to God and the type of regular fellowship we will have with Jesus and other

believers throughout history. (Keep in mind, there will be billions of redeemed saints throughout the ages.) Other rewards talk about our place of authority in God's kingdom to impart life and serve all of creation. Still other rewards are related to gold, precious stones, riches, and other treasures we will have. All will experience eternal life with no more sorrow, pain, suffering, or death. However, only some will experience eternal life with great eternal riches, honor, and glory derived from the glory of God.

In the midst of God's judgments, God is incredibly gracious. David stumbled many times, but God called him a man after his own heart (Acts 13:22) willing to do everything God wanted. The Apostle Paul murdered Christians and yet God transformed him into a man who won a crown of glory. God unashamedly called himself "The Mighty One of Jacob" after Jacob wrestled with God in tears, beseeching the blessing.

Revelation 15:2 depicts those who have overcome singing the song of Moses (describing the terrible consequences of sin Jesus saved them from), and the song of the Lamb (what Jesus did to make them great forever):

"Great and marvelous are your deeds, LORD God Almighty. Just and true are your ways, King of the ages. Who will not fear you, O Lord, and bring glory to your name? For you alone are holy. All nations will come and worship you, for your righteous acts have been revealed." (Revelation 15:3-4).

God's judgments saved us from the fullness of sin and its eternal torment. His judgment fell at the cross to bring reconciliation. His judgments then brought rewards he inspired and empowered us to do. Filled with joy and gratitude, we get to acclaim the Lamb that was slain who is the worthy judge of heaven and earth for all eternity.

Discussion questions:

1. When you appear at the Judgment Seat of Christ, what are some questions you think Jesus may ask you on that day?

2. Describe something you overcame by the power of Jesus- did it become a source of blessing to you and other people?

3. What do you think is the role of grace in God's final evaluation of us?

4. If you could design an "eternal reward" that you want Jesus to award you with, what would it be and why?

5. What do you want Jesus to say about you (before others) on that last day? What are you doing to make this happen?

NOTES

About the author: Jess Gjerstad

Born in 1976 in Pusan South Korea, Jess Gjerstad was rescued and adopted into the United States. Jess was raised in a Christian family and grew up in the Lutheran Church.

In 1990, Jess had a life-changing encounter with Jesus Christ. This was the first of many supernatural encounters. He also began to sense a call from God to full-time occupational ministry.

In 2003, God called Jess to leave Minnesota and everything familiar to live in Kansas City. Jess joined the staff at the International House of Prayer (IHOP-KC) in 2003 where he continues to the present. In 2004, Jess earned his Masters of Divinity from Bethel Seminary in St. Paul, Minnesota.

Since then, God has sent Jess to several nations on strategic prayer assignments. Jess also travels around the United States, teaching on prayer, evangelism, and spiritual warfare. Jess's hobbies include reading, meteorology, and prayer.

If you are interested for Jess to come and speak at your church or conference, email authorjessgjerstad@gmail.com